The VOYAGEURS
and Their SONGS

Theodore C. Blegen

MINNESOTA HISTORICAL SOCIETY, ST. PAUL

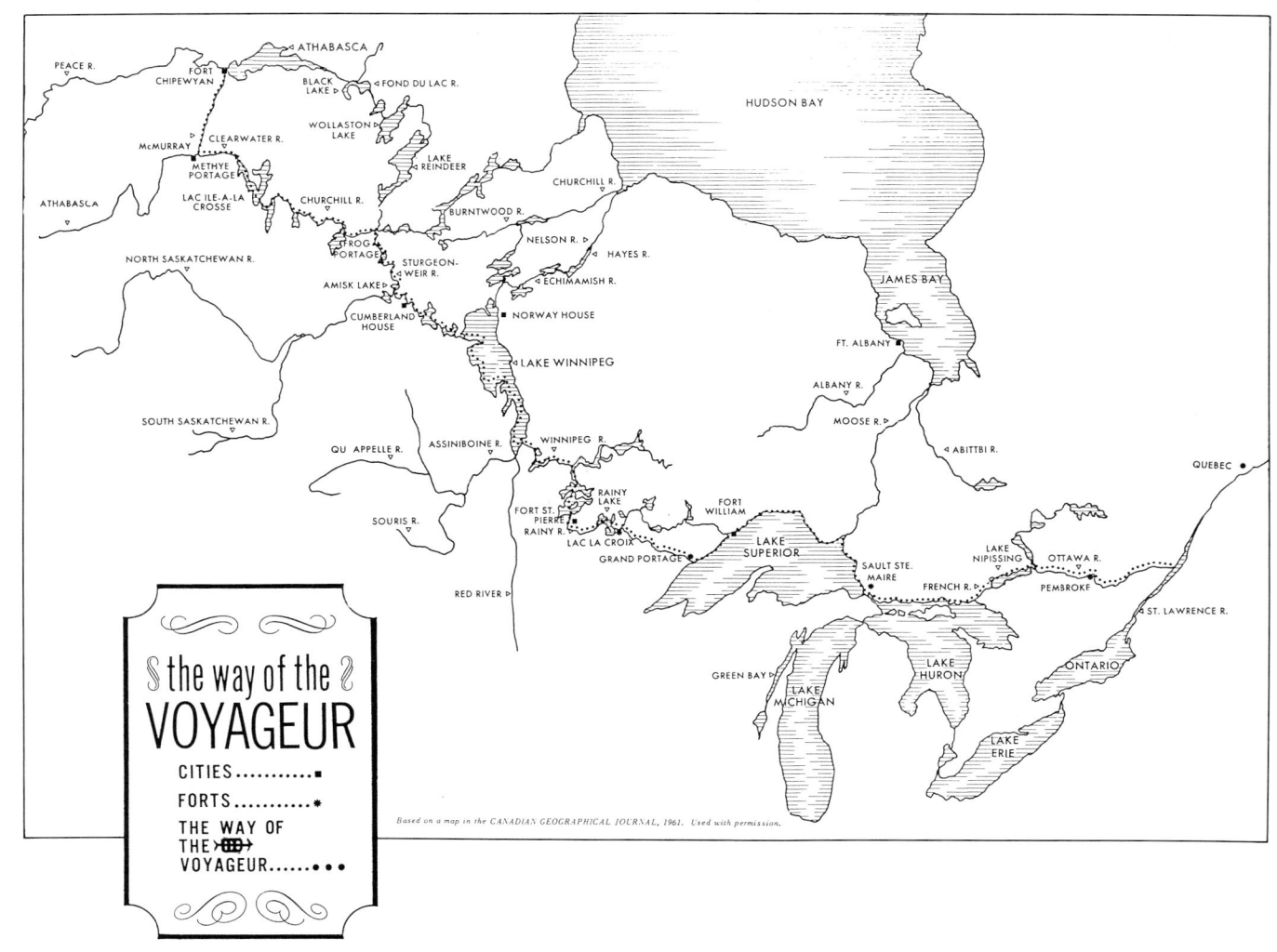

Copyright 1966 by Minnesota Historical Society
St. Paul, MN 55101
International Standard Book Number: 0-87351-029-1

10 9 8 7 6 5 4 3

The Voyageurs and Their Songs

THE VOYAGEURS were the French Canadian canoe men of the North American fur trade. They sang as they paddled birchbark canoes over the rivers and lakes of the continent from Montreal to the Pacific in the 17th, 18th, and early 19th centuries. Their songs were adapted to accompany the motion of paddles dipped in unison, and they also contributed to the morale of the paddlers. But these canoe men did not need a reason to sing. Grace Lee Nute, well-known historian of the voyageurs, points out that they sang on just about every occasion.

The fur trade canoe men came from a singing people who had carried a wealth of folk songs from Old France to New France in the 17th century. Marius Barbeau, a modern collector of such songs, writes that "in the old days" folk songs were "as familiar as barley-bread to the home-keeping villagers of Quebec, Acadia, Detroit, and Louisiana." The voyageurs, or their ancestors, came largely from the Loire Valley of France, and singing was part of their heritage. They sang while paddling a canoe or threshing grain. The women sang while spinning, weaving, or washing clothes. All French Canadians sang at play, at parties, and while dancing and drinking. They had a song for virtually every need or mood.

It is difficult to exaggerate the richness of the voyageurs' legacy of songs. A few were collected fairly early, but the vast majority of those now known were gathered in the 20th century. In 1955 the Archives of Folklore at the University of Laval in Quebec had more than 13,000 texts of French-Canadian songs. The collection testifies to the tenacity of folk memory, for nineteen out of twenty of the first harvest of songs gathered in the years after about 1916 had originally been brought across the seas from France in the 17th century. Others were created to fit the situation of the moment by the voyageurs themselves. Among this group were a number apparently too earthy for some tastes, and it is known that at least one such collection unhappily was destroyed.

The old traditional French songs, mainly unchanged through the years, were the voyageurs' favorites, and a selection of them is presented on this record. Many go on for a dozen or more verses, and those recorded here do not attempt to

A VOYAGEUR wearing the typical cap and sash. Drawing by Frederic Remington from Harper's Weekly, *February 1, 1890.*

give the complete texts. They include "A la claire fontaine," which has been called the "unofficial anthem of French Canada." It tells of a love lost because of an undelivered bouquet of roses. The voyageurs sang it as a paddling song. Perhaps the best known of these chansons is "Alouette," a strange ode to a skylark which informs the lark that the singer will pluck its head, nose, eyes, wings, tail, etc. Another popular paddling song is "En roulant ma boule" (A-rolling my ball), which sings of ponds, bonnie ducks, and a prince "on hunting bound." The ancient French ditty "A Saint-Malo," which opens this record, is also still a favorite in Quebec, where it is regarded as a patriotic song.

The voyageurs sang of simple things and events. They were fond of songs about wind and weather, spring, love, nightingales, rosebuds, cavaliers, gallant captains, and especially fair ladies. Not a few of the chansons, as you will see, had melancholy themes, but most of them could be, and were, sung robustly.

The songs have shed a glamour over the voyageurs that was deepened by their volubility, their traditionally courteous ways, and perhaps also by the inherent elegancies in the French speech, despite the fact that most voyageurs could neither read nor write. They were a gay people. They loved to talk, liked color and finery, enjoyed races and displays of prowess, and took pride in being voyageurs. And they wore picturesque clothing — red caps; bright hooded cloaks, frequently blue; braided sashes, from which hung beaded pouches packed with clay pipes, tobacco, and other possessions much valued on their long journeys. They wore leggings, deer moccasins, and plumes if their travels had taken them much beyond Lake Superior.

A prominent American fur trader of the 1830s, Henry H. Sibley, found the French Canadians "hardy, cheerful and courageous," strong, merry, good natured, and unrivaled in their mastery of canoes. Miss Nute quotes a seventy-year-old voyageur who bragged that he could "paddle, walk and sing with any man" he had ever seen. For him "no portage was ever too long." He said that he knew fifty songs, had saved ten lives, had had twelve wives and six running dogs, and had spent all his money in pleasure. "There is no life," he said, "as happy as a voyageur's life."

Emphasis on the glamour of voyageur life must not obscure for us the fact that

VOYAGEURS portaging packs which usually weighed ninety pounds each. Drawing by Frederic Remington from Harper's Weekly, *February 1, 1890.*

it was rough and hard. Normally the voyageur worked a fourteen-hour day, or longer, depending on the weather. When paddling, he was allowed a brief rest, called a "pipe," every few miles (usually three). It took stamina and muscle to paddle all day long on lakes and rivers. It took courage to run foaming rapids where one mistake could mean disaster. It required nerve and skill in appraising the weather to cut across bays in Lake Superior where storms could tear a canoe to bits. It took strong backs and steady legs to carry at a trotting pace one or more ninety-pound packs of goods or furs over portages, even though there were *poses,* or places of rest, on the longer ones.

Canoeing, with its loading, paddling, unloading, and portaging, was only part of the job of the voyageurs. They also had to be skilled in making and repairing canoes, building forts in the wilderness, and handling dog teams for winter travel. They were called upon to do any kind of physical work involved in the getting, handling, and transporting of furs.

The voyageurs were not owners, shareholders, or managers, but their skill as workmen was the foundation of the fur trade. They were essential, first in the French period when they acquired the techniques of their profession and began to master the geographical intricacies of the West; then in the British era of far-flung posts and large organizations like the Hudson's Bay Company and the North West Company; and later — south of the Canadian border — in the trade that blossomed in the United States after the War of 1812 under John Jacob Astor's American Fur Company and others. Each of these groups reached out to markets in Europe. Their products were sold at fur auctions in London and Leipzig, and prime beaver pelts were in great demand while the beaver hat maintained its popularity.

The area in which the fur trade operated was gradually enlarged from the French period until it reached the Pacific and the Arctic in the 1800s. In the British and American periods the trade expanded to the west and north, and transcontinental canoe routes were developed. (See map on inside back cover.) This meant more work for the voyageur. It increased the volume of trade goods to be transported inland for bartering with the Indians, the number of posts to be built across the land, and the amount of furs carried to market. While the voyageur had nothing to do with the complex business of financing, marketing furs, and procuring trade goods, the decisions made at high policy levels were always predicated upon his work.

There were two classes of voyageurs: the *mangeurs de lard* or pork-eaters, and the *hivernants* or winterers. The first name is derived from food, the second from voyageur life at distant posts. The pork-eaters plied the waters between Montreal and the great fur post at Grand Portage on the north shore of Lake Superior. Their food consisted of dried peas or pounded leached corn boiled in pork fat.

The winterers were voyageurs who plied the waters to the west beyond the height of land between Grand Portage and Rainy Lake from which the waters divide, running east to the Atlantic, north to the Arctic, and south to the Gulf of Mexico. The winterers were the higher caste. When a winterer crossed the height of land for the first time, a special ceremony was performed. He was sprinkled with water and made to swear certain pledges, one of which was never to kiss the wife of another voyageur without her consent. After the ceremony, he was entitled to wear a plume in his hat, a privilege pork-eaters were denied.

There were other differences between the two groups. At Grand Portage the winterers received rations of meat, bread, and wine. They were permitted to sleep in tents, while the pork-eaters slept under their overturned canoes. Both groups, however, were genuine voyageurs, both were skilled paddlers, and both sang the French songs.

The fur trade developed its techniques, personnel, and mastery of wilderness problems through more than two centuries from the 1600s to the 1800s. What one generation learned became part of the knowledge of the next. This included knowing the best water routes to the West; understanding the Indian way of life and the native languages; and all the various skills needed in handling furs.

The contribution of the Indians to the voyageurs' techniques and to western Canadian and American history is immeasurable. It was the Indians who trapped the fur-bearing animals and exchanged their skins for the traders' goods. But over and above this, the Indian way of life produced the canoe, which the white man adopted as a means of transport, and a food known as pemmican, which made the long journeys of the voyageurs possible.

Pemmican was made from pounded and dried buffalo meat, mixed with grease and often seasoned with berries. It could be eaten dry or mixed with water to make soup. Packed in buffalo-skin bags, it kept well and was readily portable. So important was this long-lasting Indian food that its manufacture was a big business in itself. Pemmican was made at fur posts in the buffalo country and distributed in ninety-pound packs to the many trading posts that dotted the wilderness.

The Algonquian birchbark canoe was an invention out of ancient Indian times. Put together without a single nail from birchbark, roots, cedar boards, and gum, it was a marvel of grace, eminently suited to voyaging by lake or by stream. It also had a capacity for carrying an almost incredible load.

Two principal sizes of canoes were used in the fur trade: large "Montreal" canoes on the broad rivers and lake expanses on the eastern end of the route, between Montreal and Lake Superior, smaller "North" canoes for the routes beyond Lake Superior. The Montreal canoe was thirty-five to forty feet in length, with paddling places for twelve or fourteen men, and a carrying capacity of five thousand pounds or more. The North canoe was shorter than the Montreal canoe by some ten feet, but it could hold a crew of eight men and a baggage load of two or three thousand pounds.

THE INTERIOR of a fur post showing Indians trading for furs. Sketch by C. W. Jefferys from the Imperial Oil Collection and The Picture Gallery of Canadian History, courtesy The Ryerson Press (Toronto, 1945).

In these fragile craft, the voyageurs began their journeys each spring, carrying goods from Montreal for distribution to posts strung across the continent to the Pacific and the Arctic or along the upper and lower Mississippi and Missouri rivers. Traveling with them might be a *bourgeois* (a partner in the North West Company), and several clerks who were to be in charge of various trading posts.

Montreal was the great employment center of the fur trade. There each spring representatives of the large companies or the independent traders hired as many voyageurs as they needed. The men signed contracts for one or more years of service at so many livres per year (ordinarily 400 for a pork-eater, more for the key posts of bowmen and steersmen). They were given certain individual supplies, including tobacco and a blanket.

The canoes were very carefully loaded with trade goods to be bartered for the Indians' furs. These goods, sent out from England, included knives and guns, shot, powder, hatchets, kettles, beads, tobacco, ribbons, mirrors, blankets, even hats — things the natives prized as wonders from an unknown world. And there were also kegs of whisky and rum, which many traders mixed with water before distributing to the Indians. Placed in the canoes also were sails, which the voyageurs used when weather conditions permitted, ropes to haul the vessels along the edges of perilous waters to save portaging, sponges for quick use against leaks, bark and other materials for mending and patching, and the personal possessions of the voyageurs, *bourgeois*, and clerks.

The point of embarkation for the fur fleets was Lachine, a few miles from Montreal above the great Lachine Rapids. The brigades, which sometimes included as many as thirty canoes, would start off at the beginning of May, red paddles flashing, songs sounding goodbys, the adventure of hundreds of miles of voyaging begun. Yet not quite begun. For there was always a ritual stop at the Church of St. Anne's on the west side of Montreal Island, where the voyageurs paused to pray for protection on the journey and to deposit coins to assure that masses would be said in their behalf. Then the trip really got under way.

The initial destination of many of the brigades leaving Montreal during the heyday of the British fur trade was the great post at Grand Portage, headquarters of the North West Company. About two months were required to make the 450-mile trip up the Ottawa and Mattawa rivers with their difficult portages, through Lake Nipissing, the French River, and around the north edge of Lake Huron to the long portage at Sault Ste. Marie at the eastern end of Lake Superior. The voyageurs paddled from dawn to nightfall, carrying the big canoes and the ninety-pound packs over portages, and sleeping on the ground with a blanket for cover. They suffered the tortures of mosquitoes, the burning glare of a hot sun on cloudless days, soaking rains, and soggy mud-laden clothes after wading through marshes up to their waists. All these and more, the short, sturdy voyageurs endured gaily, singing their way across lakes, enjoying the brief rests to smoke and eat, and sleeping soundly at night whether the winds were cold or hot.

A NORTH WEST COMPANY FUR POST. This post, surrounded by a stockade stood on Minnesota's Sandy Lake in the late 1700s. Drawing by Evan A. Hart in the collections of the Minnesota Historical Society.

A MONTREAL CANOE on Lake Superior. Colored steel engraving by Frances A. Hopkins in the Minnesota Historical Society's collections.

The climax of the trip from Montreal west was the arrival, in late June or early July, at Grand Portage. This busy, 18th-century trading post on Lake Superior, with a stockade enclosing some sixteen buildings, was a great summer emporium. At Grand Portage voyageurs and traders from east and west met. It was a rendezvous to which the traders from the northwest brought their harvests of furs and the men from Montreal landed the goods to be used in another season of barter. Here the canoes were loaded with packs of furs for the return journey to Montreal, while the men from the interior assembled their supplies for another year of trading in the West. The company's partners, or managers, were also there to consider problems of policy. The place was crowded with clerks, interpreters, pork-eaters, winterers or Nor'Westers, Indians — men, women, children — and swarms of dogs.

The voyageurs of a typical brigade — say in the early 1790s — knew that their arrival would be hailed as an exciting event. Crowds would line the dock and the beach to greet them. There would be shouts of welcome. The voyageurs, who loved a good show, usually contrived a spectacular arrival. Behind a nearby peninsula (Point de Chapeau, now called Hat Point), they landed and decked themselves out in their best finery. Then they came sweeping around the point in their canoes and headed down picturesque Grand Portage Bay, which is protected by an island that one writer has likened to "an emerald on a lady's hand mirror." Flags flew at the sterns of the canoes, paddles moved with swift precision, and the canoes flashed over the water while the paddlers sang a stirring song.

Soon the voyageurs were ashore, greeting fellow voyageurs from the deep hinterland. One can imagine the quick talk among pork-eaters and winterers, the rejoicing over a safe arrival after what everyone knew was a tough journey, partners and clerks meeting at the post, red men looking on in wonder. Here white

A NORTH CANOE passing a cliff. Note the plumes in the voyageurs' hats. Painting by Frances A. Hopkins, courtesy Public Archives of Canada.

man met white man to exchange news or to listen to stories of adventure in the wilderness; here white men and Indians mingled, and civilization met the late Stone Age.

Grand Portage in summer was a gay and busy place, full of fun, gossip, boasting, and news. The voyageurs enjoyed the excitement of crowds and the balls held in the great dining hall, where they danced reels and square dances with Indian maidens as partners. These balls went on late into the night to the music of bagpipes, fiddles, and flutes.

For the Nor'Westers from the interior, Grand Portage in summer must have seemed like a return to civilization. And from it they set off again in a few weeks for the long return journey to their posts in the interior. These men knew the far reaches of western waterways. They were old hands at portaging, and "lining", or running the rapids of northern waters, on some of which they and their comrades met tragedy — as evidenced by crosses that the voyageurs erected now and then to mark graves along the banks.

The Nor'Westers were not at all afraid of rough rapids. Eric W. Morse writes that "White water was the icing on the voyageurs' cake." In running them, much depended on the skill of the bowman and steersman, who held their positions by virtue of their experience and expertness. But accidents did happen. Canoes overturned, spilling men and baggage into a raging current. Today underwater archaeologists are using diving equipment to recover kettles, guns, and other implements lost in the rapids of northern streams nearly two centuries ago.

The western country was dotted with trading posts built in the French, British, and American eras of the trade. In Minnesota alone more than 130 such establishments have been mapped, and some sites have been excavated. The posts had

UNLOADING a North canoe at a trading post. Engraving from George M. Grant, ed., Picturesque Canada (Toronto, 1882).

protecting stockades and clusters of buildings, normally storehouses, workshops, powder magazines, and houses for the clerks and voyageurs. Throughout the autumn and winter, the clerks and their assistants lived in these outposts and traded for furs. From them in winter the voyageurs often drove dog teams pulling sleds — singing their ballads just as they did in summer while paddling. At them the voyageurs met Indian girls and often entered upon temporary or permanent marriages.

When spring came and the ice broke up on streams and lakes, the clerks and voyageurs again got busy with preparations for the trip to Grand Portage. Their furs and pelts were packed into ninety-pound bales, and when suitable weather permitted, they started on the journey. If their posts were too far away for them to make the round trip in the open season, they would go part way, and send their packs on with other traders who could reach the lake emporium and still have time enough to get back to their winter posts.

For many years prime beaver was a major goal of western fur gathering. It was used to make felt for the popular (and expensive) beaver hats. But many other kinds of furs were also collected. Early in the 1800s, in a single year, Alexander Henry the Younger sent off to Grand Portage from the Red River region the furs and pelts of 125 black bears, 49 brown bears, 4 grizzly bears, 862 wolves, 509 foxes, 125 raccoons, 322 fishers, 214 otters, 1,456 martens, 507 minks, 45 wolverines, 469 moose, and 12,470 muskrats.

The voyageurs made vital contributions to the fur trade over a period of several centuries until the mid-1800s. These contributions, in themselves, are enough to assure them a significant place in American history. But the mark of the voyageurs reaches beyond the boundaries of trade. They also played an important role in the exploration of the continent. Because of their knowledge of waterways and landways, they accompanied and aided nearly all the explorers of the western country — the surveyors, the map makers, the diplomats, the men of large fame. One could call a roll of well-known explorers from La Vérendrye and Du Lhut to Sir Alexander Mackenzie, Carver, Schoolcraft, and Nicollet — and voyageurs in every instance played parts in the deeds accomplished by these men. As Miss Nute has pointed out, the voyageurs made their "knowledge of the wilderness and its ways" freely available to the explorers "with no hope of recognition." They simply did their job — and they did it well.

Voyageurs made other contributions as soldiers; as builders of trading posts; and, after their fur trade days were over, as settlers in communities they had helped to found. They also left a heritage of French names on the North American map — names of rivers and lakes and villages and cities.

Happily, not all the voyageur contributions are silent. The lore of song, bequeathed to later generations, is one of their many contributions to Canada and the United States. The spirit of the voyageurs is evident in the chansons sung by French Canadians on this record — the very words and melodies heard on wilderness rivers and lakes in the 1700s and 1800s.

THE PARTIALLY RESTORED POST of the North West Company at Grand Portage, now within Grand Portage National Monument. Courtesy National Park Service.

VOYAGEURS around a campfire. Drawing by Frederic Remington from Harper's Weekly, February 1, 1890.

The Songs

À Saint-Malo (To Saint-Malo)

THE TITLE of this song names the famous port of Saint-Malo from which French explorer Jacques Cartier sailed to the New World in 1634. Although the title reminds French Canadians of a glorious past, the song itself has nothing to do with Cartier and very little to do with Saint-Malo. Instead it speaks of three saucy ladies who go down to the docks to bargain with a merchant for grain. They do not wish to pay his high price. "If I don't sell it," he says, "I will give it away." "À ce prix-là, on va s'arranger," they say. "At that price, one can arrange something."

1. À Saint-Malo, beau port de mer,
 À Saint-Malo, beau port de mer,
 Trois gros navires sont arrivés.
 CHORUS: Nous irons sur l'eau,
 Nous y prom-promener,
 Nous irons jouer dans l'île.

2. Chargés d'avoine, chargés de blé] 2
 Trois dames s'en vont les marchander.
 CHORUS: Nous irons sur l'eau,
 Nous y prom-promener,
 Nous irons jouer dans l'île.

3. Marchand, marchand, combien ton blé?] 2
 Trois francs l'avoine, six francs le blé.
 CHORUS: Nous irons sur l'eau,
 Nous y prom-promener,
 Nous irons jouer dans l'île.

4. C'est bien trop cher d'une bonne moitié] 2
 Montez, madame, vous le verrez.

 CHORUS: Nous irons sur l'eau,
 Nous y prom-promener,
 Nous irons jouer dans l'île.

5. Marchand d'avoine, n'a pas ton blé] 2
 Si je ne le vends je le donnerai.
 CHORUS: Nous irons sur l'eau,
 Nous y prom-promener,
 Nous irons jouer dans l'île.

6. Si je ne le vends, je le donnerai] 2
 À ce prix-là, on va s'arranger.
 CHORUS: Nous irons sur l'eau,
 Nous y prom-promener,
 Nous irons jouer dans l'île,
 dans l'île.

Envoyons de l'avant (Send her along)

THIS IS a paddling song about returning to relatives in Canada. The singers are gay as they anticipate a home-coming welcome, especially from the girls they love best, and the spirited rhythm emphasizes their impatience. Early in the evening the young ladies speak of their other beaux, but before the singers leave the girls jealously ask them about other sweethearts.

CHORUS: Envoyons de l'avant, nos gens!
 Envoyons de l'avant!
 Envoyons de l'avant, nos gens!
 Envoyons de l'avant!

1. Quand on part de chantier,
 Mes chers amis, tous le coeur gai,
 Pour aller voir tous nos parents,
 Mes chers amis, le coeur content.
 CHORUS

2. Pour aller voir tous nos parents,
   Mes chers amis, le coeur content.
   Mais qu'on arrive en Canada
   Il va falloir y mouiller ça.
   CHORUS

3. Ah! mais que ça soit tout mouillé
   Vous allez voir que ça va marcher!
   Mais que nos amis nous voyent arriver,
   Ils vont se mettre à rire, à chanter.
   CHORUS

4. Dimanche au soir, à la veillée,
   Nous irons voir nos compagnées,
   Elles vont nous dire, mais en entrant,
   Voila mon amant, j'ai le coeur content!
   CHORUS

5. Et au milieu de la veillée
   Elles vont parler de leurs cavaliers
   Elles vont nous dire, mais en partant
   As-tu fréquenté les amantes?
   CHORUS

6. Elles vont nous dire, mais en partent
   As-tu fréquenté les amantes?
   Qui a composé la chanson?
   C'est pour Blanchette, le joli garcon.
   CHORUS

C'est le vent frivolant (It is the frivolous wind)

THIS BALLAD tells of three ducks swimming in a pond behind a house. Along comes the king's son, hunting; he aims at the black duck but hits the white one. Oh, wicked son of the king! The song then goes on to tell of the white duck's death and of the three ladies who pick up its feathers which were scattered by the "frivolous wind."

REFRAIN: C'est le vent, c'est le vent
             frivolant,
         C'est le vent, c'est le vent
             frivolant.

1. Derrière chez nous y-a-t'un étang,]2
   C'est le vent, c'est le vent frivolant.]
   Trois beaux canards s'en vont baignant,
   C'est le vent, qui vole, qui frivole.
   REFRAIN

2. Trois beaux canards s'en vont
       baignant,   ]2
   C'est le vent, c'est le vent frivolant.]
   Le fils du roi s'en va chassant,
   C'est le vent, qui vole, qui frivole.
   REFRAIN

3. Visa le noir, tua le blanc,   ]2
   C'est le vent, c'est le vent frivolant.]
   O fils du roi, tu es méchant,
   C'est le vent, qui vole, qui frivole.
   REFRAIN

4. D'avoir tué mon canard blanc,   ]2
   C'est le vent, c'est le vent frivolant.]
   Par dessous l'aile il perd son sang,
   C'est le vent, qui vole, qui frivole.
   REFRAIN

5. Toutes ses plumes s'en vont au vent,]2
   C'est le vent, c'est le vent frivolant.]
   Trois dames s'en vont les ramassant,
   C'est le vent, qui vole, qui frivole.
   REFRAIN

En roulant ma boule (A-rolling my Ball)

THIS ROLLICKING "jongleur" song, like "C'est le vent frivolant," is about three beautiful ducks — "trois beaux canards" — and a prince who went hunting with his shining gun. He shot the whitest duck, and three maidens picked up the feathers. Undoubtedly the rhythm made this song popular among the paddling voyageurs, and it has remained highly popular among French Canadians to this day. More than ninety versions have been collected.

CHORUS: En roulant ma boule roulant,
        En roulant ma boule.
        En roulant ma boule roulant,
        En roulant ma boule.

1. Derrière chez nous y-a-t'un étang,]2
   En roulant ma boule,   ]
   Trois beaux canards s'en vont baignant,
   Rouli-roulant, ma boule roulant
   CHORUS

2. Le fils du roi s'en va chassant,]2
   En roulant ma boule,   ]
   Avec son grand fusil d'argent,
   Rouli-roulant, ma boule roulant
   CHORUS

3. Visa le noir, tua le blanc,]2
   En roulant ma boule,   ]
   O fils du roi, tu es méchant,
   Rouli-roulant, ma boule roulant
   CHORUS

4. D'avoir tué mon canard blanc,]2
   En roulant ma boule,   ]

Par dessous l'aile il perd son sang,
 Rouli-roulant, ma boule roulant
CHORUS

5. Et toutes ses plumes s'en vont au
    vent,
 En roulant ma boule,] 2
Trois dames s'en vont les ramassant,
 Rouli-roulant, ma boule roulant
CHORUS

6. C'est pour en faire un lit de camp,] 2
 En roulant ma boule,
Pour y coucher tous les passants,
 Rouli-roulant, ma boule roulant
CHORUS

Margoton va-t-á l'eau
(Margoton goes for water)

THIS IS the sad story of poor Margoton who went with a pitcher to an empty well, fell in, and cried for help. Three youths came riding by, heard her cries, and quite ungallantly drove a bargain with her. What would she give them if they pulled her out? Her answer was prompt and generous — a tender kiss, presumably one for each lad. But when they hauled her out, clever Margoton fled. The song ends on a teasing note: "This is the way girls catch boys."

1. Margot s'en va-t-à l'eau, avecque son
    cruchon,
 La fontaine était creuse, elle est tombée
    au fond.
  Aie, aie, aie, aie! se dit Margoton.

2. La fontaine était creuse, elle est
    tombée au fond
 Par là passèrent trois jeunes et si jolis
    garçons.
  Aie, aie, aie, aie! se dit Margoton.

3. Par là passèrent trois jeunes et si
    jolis garçons.
 Que donnerez-vous, la belle, si nous vous
    en tirerons.
  Aie, aie, aie, aie! se dit Margoton.

4. Que donnerez vous, la belle, si nous
    vous en tirerons,
 Un doux baiser, dit-elle, en guise de
    doublon.
  Aie, aie, aie, aie! se dirent les garçons.

5. Un doux baiser, dit-elle, en guise de
    doublon.

SHOOTING THE RAPIDS. Engraving from G. M. Grant, Ocean to Ocean: Sandford Fleming's Expedition through Canada in 1872 *(London, 1873).*

Et quand elle fut dehors elle tourna les talons.
Aie, aie, aie, aie! se dirent les garçons.

6. Et quand elle fut dehors elle tourna les talons.
C'est ainsi que les filles attrappent les garçons.
Aie, aie, aie, aie! se dit Margoton.
Aie, aie, aie, aie! finit la chanson.

Mon Merle (My Blackbird)

THIS CHARMING song, with enlarging repetitions, is about "my blackbird," which lost its beak, head, neck, back, wing, and tail, and it asks how one expects the poor bird to sing. The text is similar to that of "Alouette" below.

1. Mon merle a perdu son bec] 2
   Un bec, deux becs, trois becs, marlo
   CHORUS: Comment veux-tu mon merle, mon merle?
   Comment veux-tu mon merle chanter?

2. Mon merle a perdu son oeil] 2
   Un oeil, deux yeux, trois yeux,
   Un bec, deux becs, trois becs, marlo
   CHORUS

3. Mon merle a perdu sa tête] 2
   Un tête, deux têtes, trois têtes
   Un oeil, deux yeux, trois yeux,
   Un bec, deux becs, trois becs, marlo
   CHORUS

4. Mon merle a perdu son cou] 2
   Un cou, deux cous, trois cous
   Un tête, deux têtes, trois têtes
   Un oeil, deux yeux, trois yeux
   Un bec, deux becs, trois becs, marlo
   CHORUS

5. Mon merle a perdu son dos] 2
   Un dos, deux dos, trois dos
   Un cou, deux cous, trois cou
   Un tête, deux têtes, trois têtes
   Un oeil, deux yeux, trois yeux
   Un bec, deux becs, trois becs, marlo
   CHORUS

6. Mon merle a perdu son aile] 2
   Un aile, deux ailes, trois ailes
   Un dos, deux dos, trois dos
   Un cou, deux cous, trois cous
   Un tête, deux têtes, trois têtes
   Un oeil, deux yeux, trois yeux
   Un bec, deux becs, trois becs, marlo
   CHORUS

7. Mon merle a perdu sa queue] 2
   Un queue, deux queues, trois queues
   Un aile, deux ailes, trois ailes
   Un dos, deux dos, trois dos
   Un cou, deux cous, trois cous
   Un tête, deux têtes, trois têtes
   Un oeil, deux yeux, trois yeux
   Un bec, deux becs, trois becs, marlo
   CHORUS: Oh!

Dans les prisons de Nantes (In the prison of Nantes)

ONE EDITION of this song suggests that it should be sung "avec sentiment." It tells the tale of a prisoner whose only visitor was the jailor's young daughter. He asks her what his fate is to be, and she replies that rumor has it that he has only one more day to live. In several verses omitted here, the prisoner asks the daughter to let his feet "have play." She unlocks his fetters, and he proves to be a very lively lad, making his escape by sea. The last verse, included here, suggests that after his escape, the prisoner's thoughts lingered on the idea of marrying the girl if he ever returned to Nantes.

1. Dans les prisons de Nantes,] 2
   Il y-a-t'un prisonnier
   Faluron, dondaine,
   Il y-a-t'un prisonnier
   Faluron, dondé.

2. Que personne ne va voir,] 2
   Que la fille du geôlier,
   Faluron, dondaine,
   Que la fille du geôlier,
   Faluron, dondé.

3. Un jour il lui demande,] 2
   Qu'est ce que l'on dit de moué [moi]?
   Faluron, dondaine,
   Qu'est ce que l'on dit de moué?
   Faluron, dondé.

4. Le bruit court dans la ville,] 2
   Que demain vous mourrez,
   Faluron, dondaine,
   Que demain vous mourrez,
   Faluron, dondé.

5. Le garçon fort alerte,] 2
   À la mer s'est jeté,
   Faluron, dondaine,
   À la mer s'est jeté,
   Faluron, dondé.

6. Si je retourne à Nantes,] 2
   Oui, je l'épouserai,
   Faluron, dondaine,
   Oui, je l'épouserai,
   Faluron, dondé.

Passant par Paris (On the way to Paris)

THIS LIVELY drinking song tells of a friend of the singer who, while emptying a bottle, whispers to him that wine is good, good. The good wine puts me to sleep, says the refrain, and love wakes me up again. This refrain punctuates the singer's story about going to his sweetheart's house and finding a rival there. He tells the rival to leave; he will never get from the sweetheart what the singer himself got, namely, "the most beautiful flowers" of her heart.

1. Passant par Paris, pour y vider
      bouteille,] 2
   Un de mes amis il me dit à l'oreille:
   CHORUS: Gai, Bon, Bon,
         Le bon vin m'endort et l'amour
         m'y réveille.] 2

2. Viens-tu avec moi pour y voir la
      belle?] 2
   J'ai pris mon cheval et ma bride et ma
      selle.
   CHORUS

3. Je m'en suis allé au logis de la
      belle.] 2
   J'aperçu rival, un rival auprès d'elle.
   CHORUS

4. Je lui dis: Gallant, retire-toi d'elle,] 2
   Tu n'auras jamais ce que j'ai eu d'elle.
   CHORUS

5. Tu n'auras jamais ce que j'ai eu
      d'elle,] 2
   J'ai eu de son coeur les fleurs les plus
      belles.
   CHORUS

Au Cabaret (To the Cabaret)

THE SONG tells the mock-pathetic story of a man whose wife tries to beat him the day after they were married. So off he goes to the tavern to drink with his friends. But soon he sees his wife coming and asks his companions not to drink so much. The wife promptly finds him, calls him a drunkard, and orders him out of the cabaret. "Oh, yes," he says, "I will go when I have finished drinking." But she tells him to march straight home. In verses omitted here, the wife says that he drank a hundred times more than his income, and that he had no buttons on his coat but thirty on his nose. He then threatens to take a broomstick to her. The music parodies early church songs, lending a pseudo-tragic note to this essentially comic tale.

1. Le lendemain que je me suis marié,] 2
   Ma femme a voulu me battre.
   Au cabaret je me suis en allé
      Trouver mes amis pour boire,
   Trouver mes amis] 3
      Pour boire.

2. Mes chers amis, ne buvons pas tant,] 2
   Car je voix venir ma femme.
   Elle est là bas, elle est sur ces côtes.
      Je l'entends déjà qui gronde,
   Je l'entends déjà] 3
      Qui gronde.

3. Bien promptement elle vient au
      cabaret,   ] 2
   "Sors d'ici, ivrogne du diable!"
   "Du cabaret, ah oui! j'en sortirai,
      Quand j'aurai fini de boire,
   Quand j'aurai fini] 3
      De boire."

4. "Mon cher mari, ah! si tu continues,] 2
   Tu feras périr ta famille!
   Un pied chaussé, et puis, l'autre nu.
      File à la maison, ivrogne!
   File à la maison] 3
      Ivrogne!"

À la claire fontaine (By the clear running fountain)

THIS BALLAD of love and roses has been called the "unofficial anthem" of the French Canadians. It describes a young man who wanders by a clear fountain one summer day and hears a nightingale singing. Sing, nightingale, he says, for you have no cares while I weep because my love wanted a bouquet of roses, and I refused to give it to her. Now my love is gone. The voyageurs undoubtedly liked the song for its rhythm and for its nostalgic mood.

REFRAIN: Lui y a longtemps que je t'aime,
Jamais je ne t'oublierai.

1. A la claire fontaine,
   M'en allant promener,
   J'ai trouve l'eau si belle
   Que je m'y suis baigne.
   REFRAIN

2. Sous les feuilles d'un chêne,
   Je me suis fait sécher,
   Sur la plus haute branche
   Le rossignol chantait.
   REFRAIN

3. Chante, rossignol, chante,
   Toi qui as le coeur gai,
   Tu as le coeur à rire,
   Moi, je l'ai a pleurer.
   REFRAIN

4. Tu as le coeur à rire,
   Moi, je l'ai a pleurer,
   J'ai perdu ma maîtresse
   Sans l'avoir mérité.
   REFRAIN

5. J'ai perdu ma maîtresse
   Sans l'avoir mérité
   Pour un bouquet de roses
   Que je lui refusai.
   REFRAIN

C'est l'aviron (It's the oars!)

THERE MAY seem to be a little lack of logic in a song that tells of a ride from the seaport of La Rochelle, France, and then pitches into a lusty chorus about pulling on the oars, but it was not unusual for transplanted Frenchmen to adapt their native songs to fit their New World occupations. The voyageurs sang this as they paddled. The text explains how a young man chooses the loveliest of three girls, takes her on his horse a long way, and — at her request for a drink — stops at a fountain. The young lady refuses to drink here; later, at her father's home, she drinks many glasses, toasting her parents, her brothers and sisters, and — finally — her lover.

1. M'en revenant de la jolie Rochelle,
   M'en revenant de la jolie Rochelle,
   J'ai rencontré trois jolies demoiselles.
   CHORUS: C'est l'aviron qui nous mène, qui nous mène,
   C'est l'aviron qui nous mène en haut.

2. J'ai rencontré trois jolies demoiselles;] 2
   J'ai point choisi, mais j'ai pris la plus belle.
   CHORUS

3. J'ai point choisi, mais j'ai pris la plus belle;] 2
   J'y fis monter derrière moi, sur ma selle.
   CHORUS

4. J'y fis cent lieues sans parler avec elle;] 2
   Au bout de cent lieues, elle me demandit à boire.
   CHORUS

5. Je l'ai menée auprès d'une fontaine;] 2
   Quand elle fut là, elle ne voulut point boire.
   CHORUS

6. Je l'ai menée au logis de son père;] 2
   Quand elle fut là, elle buvait à pleins verres.
   CHORUS

7. À la santé de son père et sa mère;] 2
   À la santé de ses soeurs et ses frères.
   CHORUS

8. À la santé de ses soeurs et ses frères;] 2
   À la santé de celui que son coeur aime.
   CHORUS

Alouette (Lark)

EVERYBODY in Canada, and many people elsewhere, know "Alouette, gentle Alouette." Similar to "Mon Merle," this song concerns a lark, rather than a blackbird, which is informed by the singer that he will pluck its head, eyes, beak, back, and neck. The song has many more verses than those sung here. Canadian soldiers during World War I, it is said, carried the song back to

Laboratory Investigations in
GEOMETRY

PHARES G. O'DAFFER   STANLEY R. CLEMENS

ADDISON-WESLEY PUBLISHING COMPANY

Menlo Park, California • Reading, Massachusetts
London • Amsterdam • Don Mills, Ontario • Sydney

This book is in the
ADDISON-WESLEY INNOVATIVE SERIES

Copyright © 1976 by Addison-Wesley Publishing Company, Inc.
Philippines copyright 1976 by Addison-Wesley Publishing Company, Inc.

All rights reserved. No part of this publication may be reproduced, stored in a retrieval system, or transmitted, in any form or by any means, electronic, mechanical, photocopying, recording, or otherwise, without prior written permission of the publisher. Printed in the United States of America. Published simultaneously in Canada.

ISBN 0-201-05421-3

KL-ML-898

Introduction

In recent years the authors of geometry texts have placed a strong emphasis on definitions, correct terminology, and on the formal, axiomatic aspects of geometry. We feel that definitions and deduction are important and necessary, but that something has been lost in the process of focusing almost exclusively on the factual and on the deductive process. Geometrical relationships are often discovered inductively. Once they are discovered, it is the deductive process that is used for logical verification. To deprive students of the opportunity for extensive experience in the inductive discovery of geometrical relationships is to stifle their growth in utilizing an important mathematical process. Using deduction exclusively also can contribute to the development of a narrow view of geometry and can limit the student's ability to see the creative, interesting aspects of the subject.

Thus it is our view that a deductive approach to geometry must be undergirded and supplemented with numerous concrete exploratory experiences.

These *Laboratory Investigations in Geometry* are designed to provide such experiences and to supplement a variety of different courses in geometry. For a formal, deductive course, they can be used to provide the concrete basis for the more abstract presentation of geometric ideas. They can also provide inductive experiences to help the student discover many of the theorems that he will later prove.

In an informal course, the investigations can be used to extend the opportunities for learning new concepts and discovering new generalizations. Also, the workbook format of the investigations provides the graph paper, templates, net patterns, and cutouts which can enrich the informal course with a minimum of teacher acquisition of materials.

The investigations are designed to encourage student exploration—on an individual or group basis—using constructions, graph paper, paper folding, measurement, Miras, and a variety of other investigative techniques. Interesting topics such as the golden ratio, tangram puzzle, star polygons, symmetry, tessellations, kaleidoscopes, polyhedra, motion geometry, and the Mobius Band provide the basis for these investigations. They are not only motivational but they serve as vehicles for clarification and extension of the more basic ideas of geometry.

Students who have completed these investigations often report that they have a new confidence in their ability to "figure things out" in geometry. They say their attitude toward mathematics has improved and they have a much broader perception of what geometry is all about. If this can happen to other students, at various levels in their study of geometry, then our goals for the preparation of these investigations are in the process of being realized.

— The Authors

Suggestions for Using This Book

The investigations in this book can be used in a variety of ways. One might consider a continuum starting with exclusive use of the investigations to develop an informal course and ending with a situation in which the investigations are used only incidently. Here are some of the possibilities.

I. The investigations could serve as a basis for a complete informal course in geometry. A lesson format such as this could be used in structuring the course:
   A. Investigation
   B. Discussion
   C. Utilization
   D. Extension

Thus the students could engage in one of the investigations to begin a lesson. As the students work on the investigation it is the job of the instructor to
(a) ask penetrating questions and give leading suggestions when necessary.
(b) to communicate that learning sometimes involves making mistakes.
(c) to emphasize that a "good" question or conjecture is often as valuable as a "good" answer.
(d) to encourage individual or group participation in completing the investigation.
(e) to play the consulting role of possessor of knowledge rather than the imposing view of professor of knowledge.

During the discussion phase the ideas of the investigation can be shaped and elaborated upon. The instructor might want to develop and discuss further related ideas of geometry at this time. During the utilization phase the instructor might want to give selected exercises using the ideas developed. Finally, the problem at the bottom of each investigation could be used as an extension of the ideas of the lesson.

II. The investigations could be used in various situations where selected units of work were desired for a workshop, a seminar, or to extend a regular course. A set of investigations could be selected, and used as in I to develop the geometric ideas.

III. The investigations could also be used to *supplement* a formal, deductive course in geometry. In this case they could be utilized at various places in the course to provide:
   (a) a physical, concrete basis for later development of abstract ideas.
   (b) a vehicle for student discovery of relationships to be later proven in the course.
   (c) a source of motivation and recreation.
   (d) a means of broadening a student's perception of geometry.

IV. The investigations could be used to supplement an informal course in geometry. In this case they could be utilized at various places in the course to provide:
   (a) an additional source of motivation and recreation.
   (b) a source of preliminary exploration of ideas to be introduced.
   (c) an extension of informal ideas already introduced.
   (d) a source of additional, related informal topics.
   (e) a source of materials (paper models, cutouts, graph paper, dot paper, patterns, tessellations) for completing exercises in the regular text.

V. The investigations could be used as an integral part of a mathematics activity table or center in a classroom, or in a mathematics laboratory. Individuals or groups of students could utilize these investigations along with laboratory materials as an enrichment aspect of their mathematics experience.

Finally, in using the investigations, the students should be encouraged to become involved, as much as possible, in

    (a) using physical materials, when appropriate to aid in completing the investigation.
    (b) communicating with others testing ideas, receiving feedback, altering ideas, etc.
    (c) asking questions, making conjectures, going beyond the investigation with a "what if" attitude, looking in other books, etc.

Above all, the investigations should be approached in such a way as to provide pleasure for the student and to build his confidence and interest in geometry.

A chart which correlates the investigations with topics in a number of widely used geometry texts is available free from:

> Addison-Wesley Publishing Company
> 2725 Sand Hill Road
> Menlo Park, California 94025

— The Authors

TABLE OF CONTENTS

PUZZLES AND DISSECTIONS

Investigation 1: *The Golden Rectangle* — Page 1
Students experience the Golden Rectangle by making esthetic judgements, by measuring, and by calculating ratios.

Investigation 2: *The Golden Ratio in the Pentagram* — 2
Students discover several instances of the Golden Ratio by measuring a pentagram figure which is inscribed in a regular pentagon.

Investigation 3: *Pythagorean Theorem* — 3
Students use paper cutouts to illustrate the validity of and devise a proof for the Pythagorean Theorem.

Investigation 4: *Boats and Bridges with the Tangram Puzzle* — 5
Students gain practice in space visualization and area comparisons by constructing boat and bridge figures with the tangram puzzle.

Investigation 5: *Letters of the Alphabet and the Tangram Puzzle* — 7
Students gain additional experience with the tangram puzzle by constructing letters of the alphabet with seven pieces.

Investigation 6: *Convex Polygons from the Tangram Puzzle* — 9
Students construct the 12 nonsquare convex polygons which can be made with the tangram pieces. Often moving a single piece transforms one polygon shape to another.

Investigation 7: *Dissections of a Square* — 13
Students explore seven different dissection puzzles of the square. The pieces in each puzzle can be rearranged to form a familiar polygon shape.

Investigation 8: *Dissections of the Regular Hexagon and Dodecagon* — 17
Students discover that the regular hexagon and dodecagon can be dissected into pieces which can be rearranged to form several smaller hexagons and dodecagons.

Investigation 9: *Dissections of the Six-Pointed Star* — 19
Students explore two different dissections of a six-pointed star whose pieces can be rearranged to form three smaller six-pointed stars.

POLYGONS AND SYMMETRY

Investigation 10: *Segments on Geoboards* — 21
Students discover the number of segments of different length on geoboards of various sizes. This activity can be treated as an application of the Pythagorean Theorem.

Investigation 11: *Triangles and Quadrilaterals* — 23
Students explore the number of differently shaped triangles and quadrilaterals which can be formed on a geoboard with 3 nails on a side. They also gain practice computing areas without applying formulas.

Investigation 12: *Irregular Polygons on the Geoboard* — 25
Students search for polygons with n^2 sides on geoboards with n nails on a side.

Investigation 13: *Regular Polygons* — 27
Students discover the number of regular polygons that can be constructed on circular geoboards of various sizes.

Investigation 14: *Star Polygons* — 28
Students become familiar with the concept of star polygons by finding how many different star polygons can be constructed on an 18-nail circle geoboard.

Investigation 15: *Star Polygons* — 29
Students continue to explore star polygons by finding those that can be constructed on a 24-nail circle geoboard, and by searching for the size of the vertex angles.

Investigation 16: *Pentominoes* — 30
Students gain practice discovering and organizing counting strategies and spatial relationships as they try to find all 12 pentominoe shapes.

Investigation 17: *Symmetry of the Pentominoes* — 31
Students use the pentominoe shapes to study line reflection symmetry and rotational symmetry.

Investigation 18: *Symmetry Patterns* — 32
Students explore reflectional and rotational symmetry by completing circular figures to satisfy certain symmetry conditions.

Investigation 19: *Symmetry Pattern* — 33
Students construct a symmetry pattern and contemplate how altering the design changes its symmetry.

Investigation 20: *Rotational Symmetry on a Geoboard* — 34
Students gain practice in recognizing rotational symmetry and in developing classification strategies as they search for the 24 patterns that satisfy a certain set of conditions.

Investigation 21: *Hexominoes* — 37
Students acquire additional experiences with spatial relationships and classification schemes as they search for the 35 hexominoes.

Investigation 22: *Hexiamonds* — 39
Students discover all the hexiamond shapes.

Investigation 23: *A Theorem for Quadrilaterals* — 41
Students search for a relationship concerning the midpoints of the sides of a quadrilateral.

Investigation 24: *Angle Trisectors of a Triangle* — 42
Students search for a relationship concerning the adjacent angle trisectors of a triangle.

Investigation 25: *Three Special Points of a Triangle* — 43
Students search for a relationship concerning the centroid, the orthocenter, and the circumcenter of a triangle.

		Page
Investigation 26:	*Nine Interesting Points*	45

Students search for a relationship among nine familiar points of a triangle.

Investigation 27: *A Theorem for Triangles*   46

Students search for a relationship that involves the construction of equilateral triangles on each side of a given triangle.

Investigation 28: *A Theorem for Triangles*   47

Students search for a relationship between the altitude of an equilateral triangle and several other lengths.

Investigation 29: *A Theorem for Parallelograms*   48

Students search for a relationship that involves the construction of squares on the sides of a parallelogram.

TESSELLATIONS

Investigation 30: *Tessellations with Regular Polygons*   49

Students experiment with cutouts to determine which regular polygons tessellate the plane.

Investigation 31: *Tessellations of Triangles and Quadrilaterals*   51

Students experiment with cutouts to determine which triangles and quadrilaterals tessellate the plane.

Investigation 32: *Tessellations of Triangles and Quadrilaterals*   53

Students gain experience with spatial relationships as they draw several tessellations on dot paper.

Investigation 33: *Tessellations of Pentominoes*   55

Students experiment with several pentominoe shapes to determine whether or not tessellations can be drawn.

Investigation 34: *Tessellations of Letters of the Alphabet*   57

Students experience geometric relationships as they draw on dot paper tessellations of polygons shaped like the letters *H* and *F*.

Investigation 35: *Tessellations of Hexominoes*   59

Hexominoes, like pentominoes, are interesting polygon figures. Students draw on dot paper tessellations of several hexominoes.

Investigation 36: *Tessellations with Combinations of Regular Polygons*   61

Students find combinations of regular polygons that completely surround a vertex and use this information to search for tessellations formed by several regular polygons.

Investigation 37: *Dual Tessellation of a Regular Tessellation*   65

Students are introduced to the concept of dual tessellation.

Investigation 38: *Dual Tessellation of Triangles*   66

Students explore the concept of dual tessellation as they draw the dual of a tessellation of triangles.

Investigation 39: *Dual Tessellation of a Semiregular Tessellation*   67

Students draw the dual of a semiregular tessellation and compute the perimeter of the polygons in the dual.

Investigation 40: *Dual Tessellation of a Semiregular Tessellation*   68

Students draw the dual of a semiregular tessellation and compute the area of the polygons in the dual.

Investigation 41: *Reflectional Symmetry of a Tessellation*   69

Students study a semiregular tessellation and identify lines of reflectional symmetry.

Investigation 42: *Rotational Symmetry of a Tessellation*   70

Students study a semiregular tessellation and identify centers of rotational symmetry

Investigation 43: *Coloring Tessellations*   71

Students experience the concept of pattern as they color tessellations in special ways.

Investigation 44: *Coloring Tessellations*   72

Students consider an interesting combinatorial question while coloring a semiregular tessellation.

Investigation 45: *Coloring Tessellations*   73

Students consider another interesting combinatorial question while coloring a semiregular tessellation.

Investigation 46: *Coloring Tessellations*   74

Students use the medium of coloring a tessellation to explore reflectional symmetry.

Investigation 47: *Symmetry Properties of Tessellations*   75

Students discover how coloring a tessellation can change its symmetry properties.

Investigation 48: *Tessellations of Pentagons*   77

Students discover how a large number of pentagon tessellations can be derived from tessellations of triangles.

Investigation 49: *Tessellations of Pentagons*   78

Students discover how a pentagon tessellation can be obtained as a dual tessellation.

Investigation 50: *More Tessellations of Pentagons*   79

Students discover a simple method of deriving a pentagon tessellation from a tessellation of squares.

Investigation 51: *Tessellations of Hexagons*   80

Students discover how a large number of hexagon tessellations can be derived from a tessellation of quadrilaterals.

		Page
Investigation 52:	*Tessellations of Hexagons*	81

Students discover how hexagon tessellations can be obtained by adjoining neighboring quadrilaterals in a tessellation of quadrilaterals.

Investigation 53: *More Tessellations of Hexagons* — 82

Students discover how hexagon tessellations can be obtained from a tessellation of parallelograms.

Investigation 54: *Tessellations of Curved Figures* — 83

Students discover one method of constructing simple Escher-like tessellations of curved figures.

Investigation 55: *Tessellations of Curved Figures* — 84

Students explore methods for creating Escher-like tessellations.

Investigation 56: *Tessellations and the Construction of Dissection Puzzles* — 85

Students discover a method for generating many dissection puzzles. This investigation shows how a letter H can be cut up so that the pieces can be rearranged to form a parallelogram.

Investigation 57: *Vertex Figure Tessellation* — 86

Students explore how a tessellation can be created by drawing all vertex figures of a given tessellation.

Investigation 58: *Three-Mirror Kaleidoscope Tessellations* — 87

Students explore how a semiregular tessellation can be generated with a three-mirror kaleidoscope.

Investigation 59: *Creating Tessellations* — 88

Students are given the opportunity to create on dot paper a tessellation of their own design.

POLYHEDRA

Investigation 60: *Constructing Regular Polyhedra* — 89

Students are provided with templates for making polygon faces which can be joined with rubber bands to form regular polyhedra.

Investigation 61: *Constructing Semiregular Polyhedra* — 91

Students are provided a template for a regular hexagon which can be combined with the faces from Investigation 60 to make semiregular polyhedra.

Investigation 62: *Constructing Deltahedra* — 93

Students are provided with an equilateral triangular template which can be used to make examples of the polyhedra called deltahedra.

Investigation 63: *Pop-up Dodecahedron* — 95

Students are provided with a net and directions for making an easily constructed dodecahedron which has motivational characteristics.

Investigation 64: *Constructing a Tetrahedron* — 97

Students are provided with a pattern and directions for the easy construction of a tetrahedron.

Investigation 65: *Opposite Vertices, Edges, and Faces for Polyhedra* — 99

Students are led to count the number of opposite vertices, edges, and faces of the regular polyhedra.

Investigation 66: *Symmetry of the Cube* — 100

Students are given practice in sketching planes of symmetry and axes of rotational symmetry of the cube.

Investigation 67: *Tetrahedron, Cube, and Octahedron* — 101

Students are provided nets for construction of the tetrahedron, cube, and octahedron.

Investigation 68: *Dodecahedron* — 103

Students are provided a net for construction of a regular dodecahedron.

Investigation 69: *Icosahedron* — 105

Students are provided a net for construction of a regular icosahedron.

Investigation 70: *Tetrahedron Puzzle* — 107

Students are provided with a net for a polyhedron, two copies of which can be joined to form a tetrahedron.

Investigation 71: *Cube Puzzle* — 109

Students are provided with a net for a polyhedron, two copies of which can be joined to form a cube.

REFLECTIONS

Investigation 72: *Mira Constructions* — 111

Students are provided a worksheet which will aid them in becoming familiar with the Mira.

Investigation 73: *Mira Constructions* — 112

Students experiment with the Mira and discover several basic constructions.

Investigation 74: *Products of Reflections (Flips)* — 113

Students explore and discover a single motion which is equivalent to a product of two reflections when the lines of reflection are parallel.

Investigation 75: *Products of Reflections (Flips)* — 114

Students explore and discover a single motion that is equivalent to a product of two reflections when the lines of reflection are not parallel.

Investigation 76: *Products of Reflections (Flips)* — 115

Students are given a pair of congruent triangles and are led to discover a pair of reflection lines.

Investigation 77: *Products of Reflections (Flips)* — 117

Students are given a pair of congruent triangles and are led to discover reflection lines.

Investigation 78: *Mobius Band* — 119

Students discover several of the interesting properties possessed by the Mobius Band.

Investigation 79: *Missing Unit* — 121

Students experiment with a dissection puzzle which appears to be paradoxical.

1   THE GOLDEN RECTANGLE

Select the rectangle that you feel has the most esthetically pleasing shape.

The famous Golden Rectangle is the rectangle with length-to-width ratio approximately 1.618 (the Golden Ratio) and is often said to be the rectangle with the most pleasing shape. Use a millimeter ruler and find the length-to-width ratio for each of the rectangles above. Did you select the Golden Rectangle?

PROBLEM: If rectangle ABCD is a Golden Rectangle and rectangle AEFD is a square, show that rectangle EBCF is also a Golden Rectangle. (Hint: Use the actual value of the Golden Ratio, which is

$$\frac{1 + \sqrt{5}}{2},$$

rather than the approximation 1.618.)

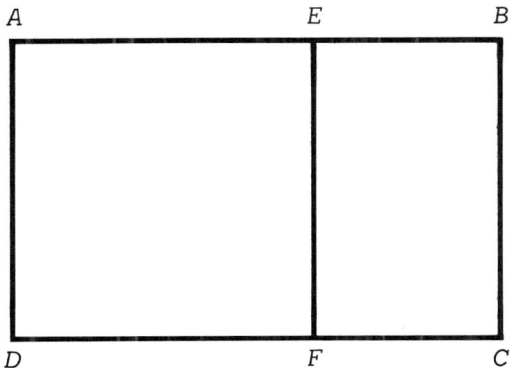

All rights reserved. Addison-Wesley Publishing Company

2   THE GOLDEN RATIO IN THE PENTAGRAM

There are segments of four different lengths in this figure.
Measure them with a millimeter ruler and compare their lengths.
How many instances of the Golden Ratio appear to occur among these ratios?

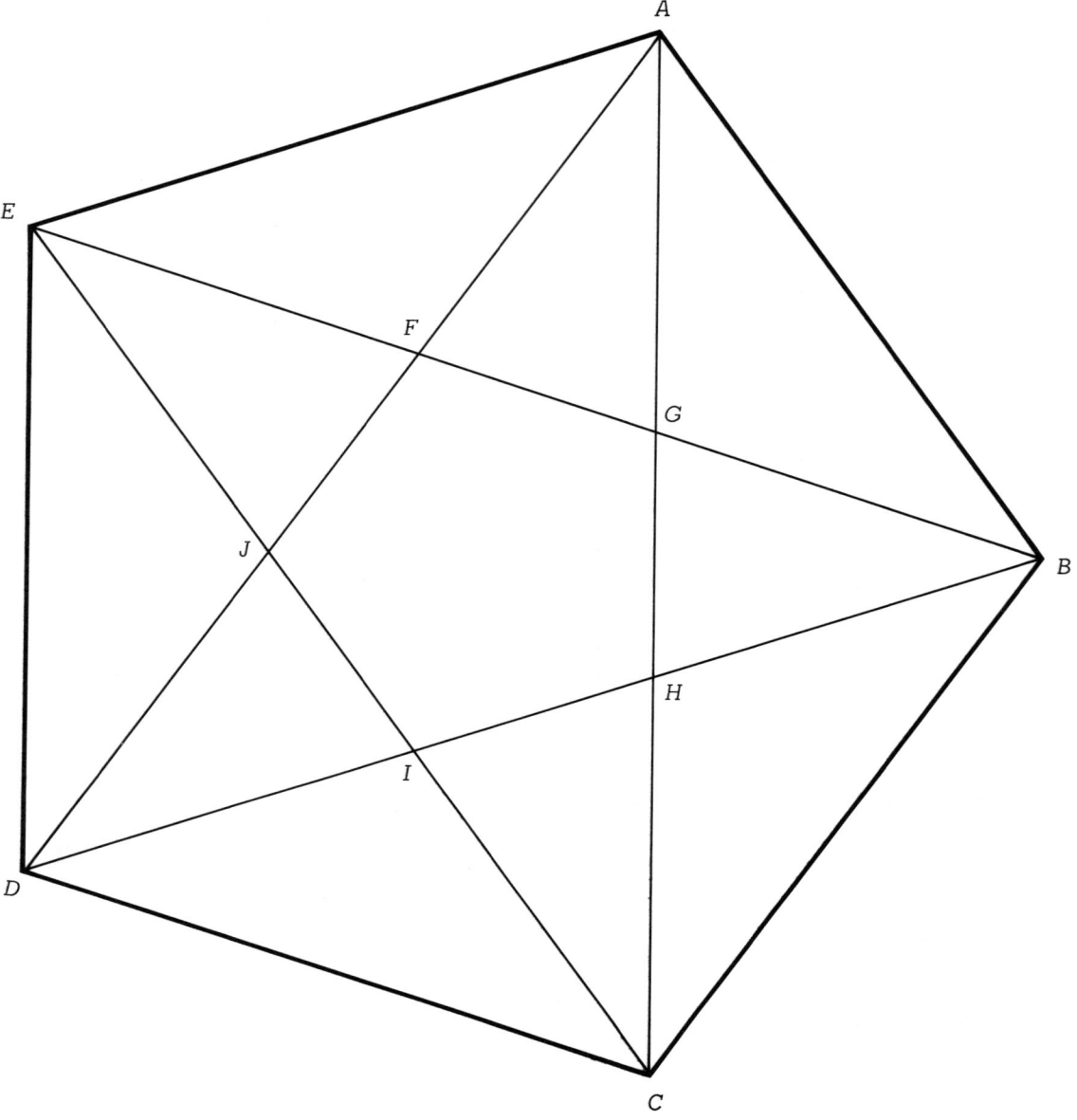

PROBLEM: Prove the $\triangle EBC$ is similar to $\triangle BHG$. From this conclude that

$$\frac{BH}{BC} = \frac{BC}{1},$$

which is equivalent to $(BC)^2 = BH$. Thus BC is the mean proportional to BH and BD.

3   PYTHAGOREAN THEOREM

Recall that the Pythagorean Theorem states that the square on the hypotenuse of a right triangle has area equal to the sum of the areas of the squares on the other two sides.

Demonstrate the validity of their theorem by cutting out the two small squares (also cut along the broken lines) and arranging the pieces on the large square.

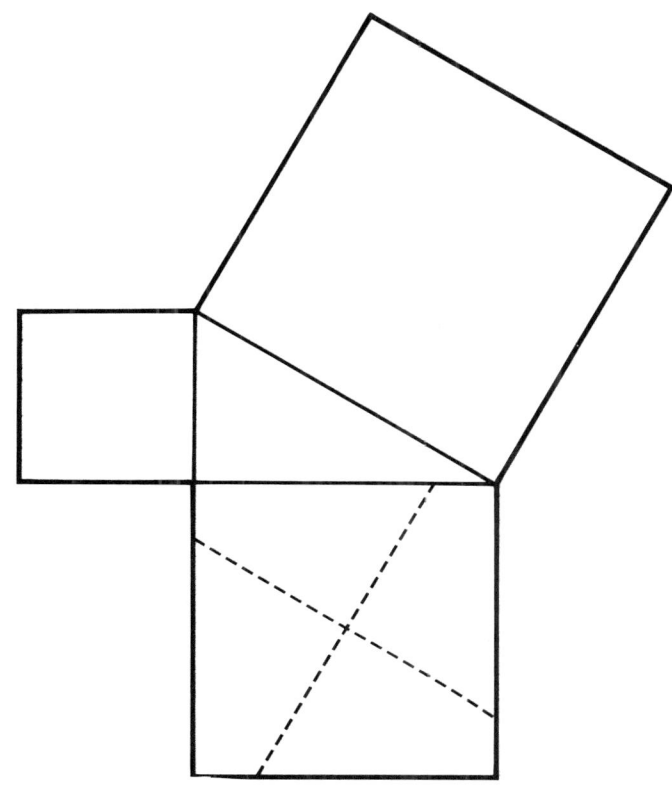

PROBLEM: Cut out 4 copies of the triangle below and arrange them as indicated to form a square. Explain how from this arrangement we can conclude that

$$(b - a)^2 + 4(½)ab = c^2.$$

Show that this equation is algebraically equivalent to

$$a^2 + b^2 = c^2.$$

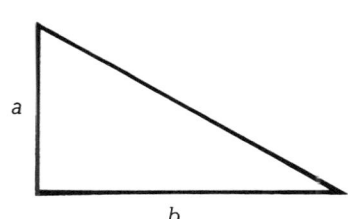

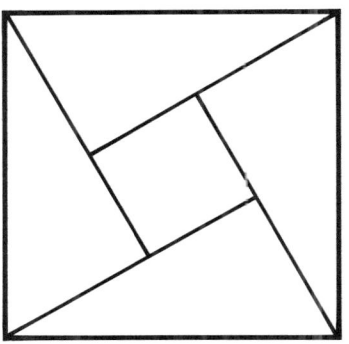

4   BOATS AND BRIDGES WITH THE TANGRAM PUZZLE

We see here how the tangram puzzle pieces can be arranged to form a boat or a bridge.

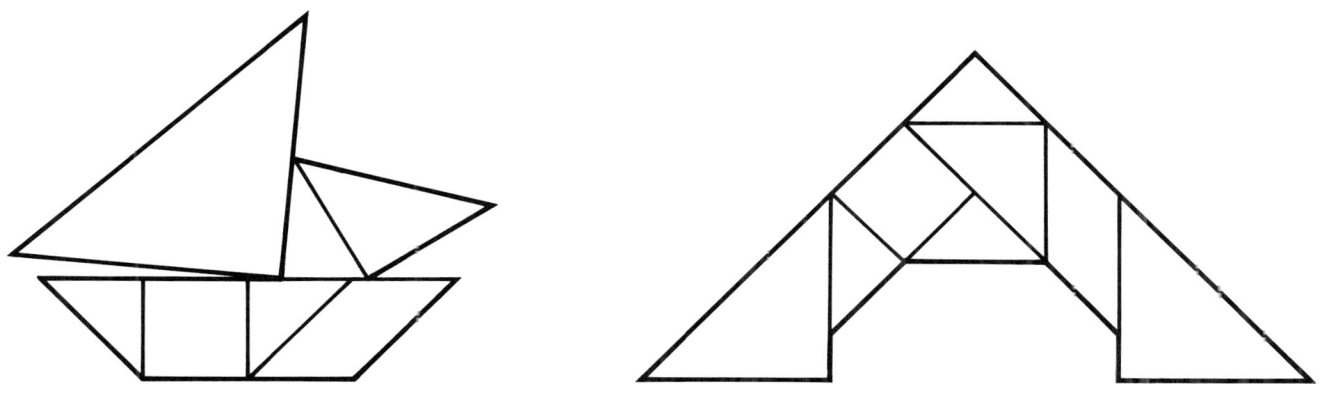

Cut out the pieces of the tangram puzzle and create with them your own boat and bridge (different from the one above).

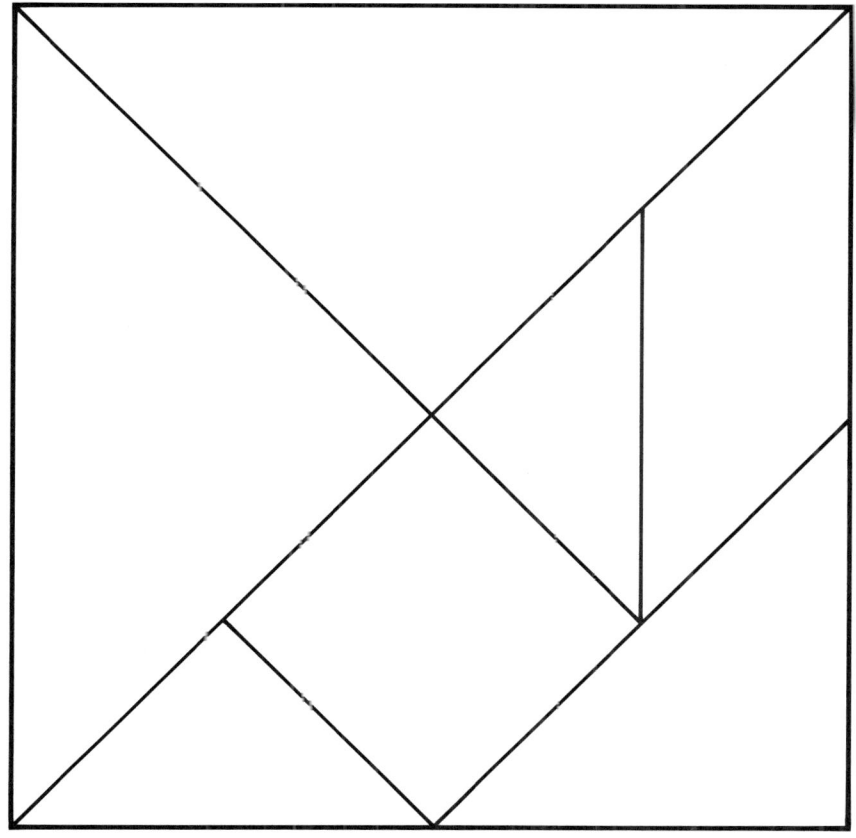

PROBLEM: If the area of the smallest triangle of the tangram puzzle is 1, what is the area of each of the other pieces of the puzzle?

5 LETTERS OF THE ALPHABET AND THE TANGRAM PUZZLE

Cut out the tangram pieces and arrange them to form the letters C and H as below.

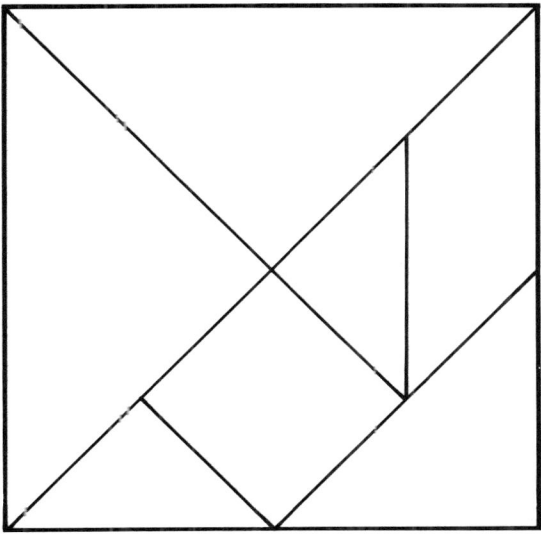

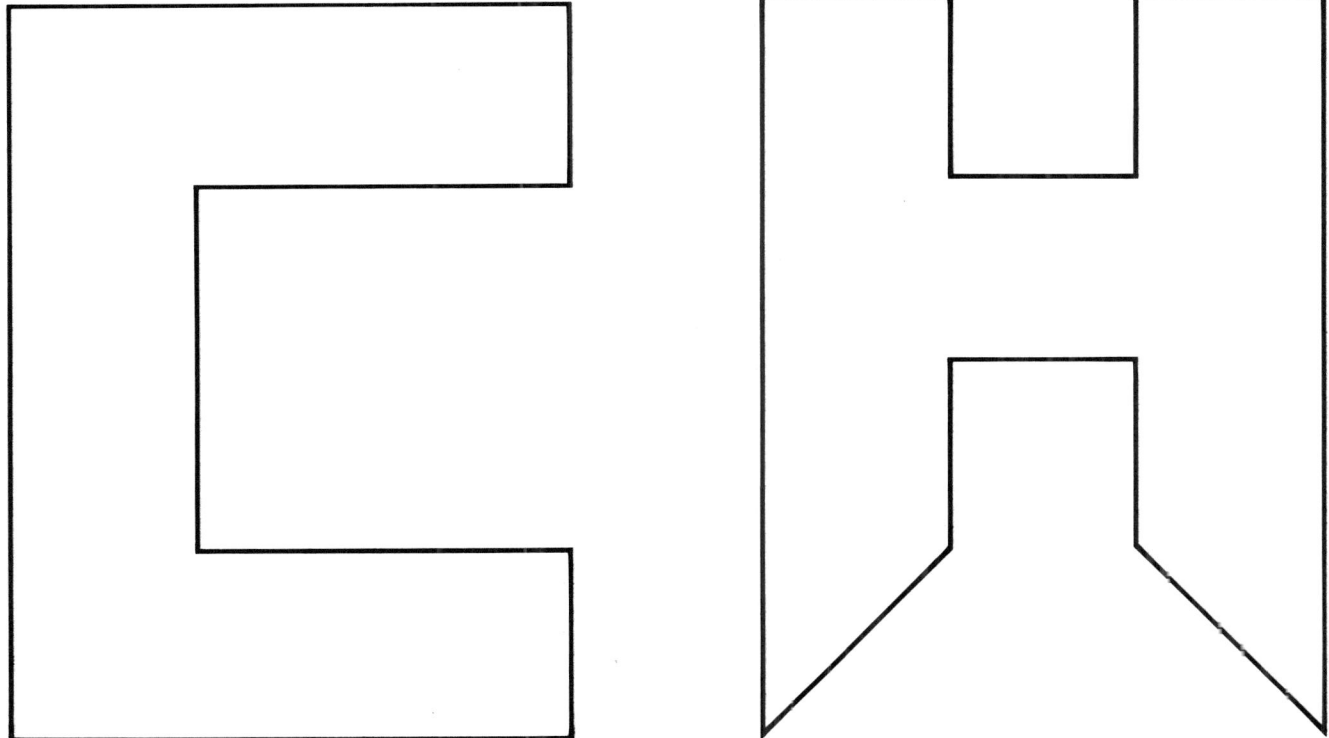

6 CONVEX POLYGONS FROM THE TANGRAM PUZZLE

In addition to a square, there are exactly 12 convex polygon shapes that can be formed with the tangram puzzle pieces. Cut out the puzzle pieces and arrange them to form each of the polygon shapes provided on the following pages. Draw your solution in each polygon.

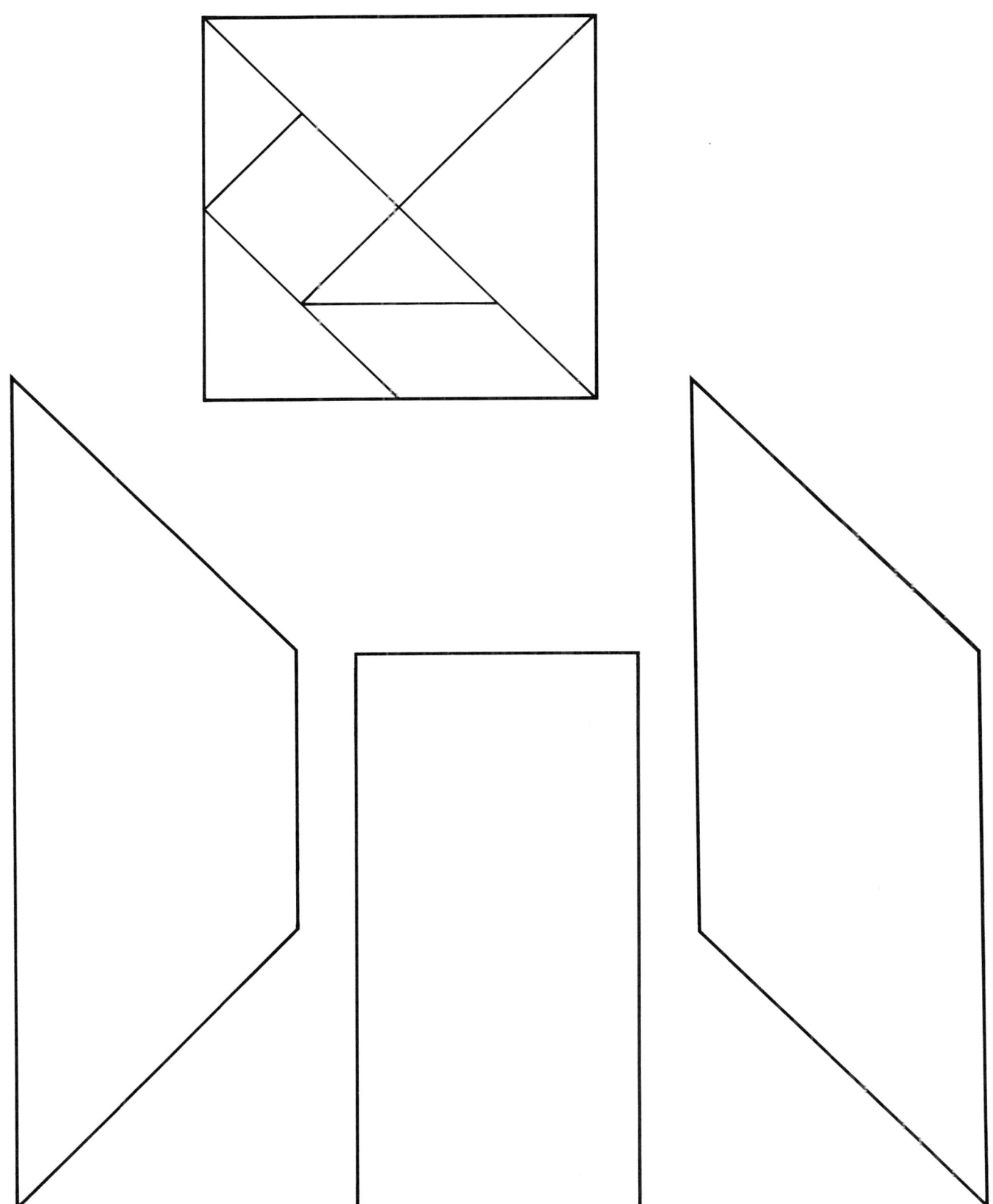

CONVEX POLYGONS FROM THE TANGRAM PUZZLE (continued)

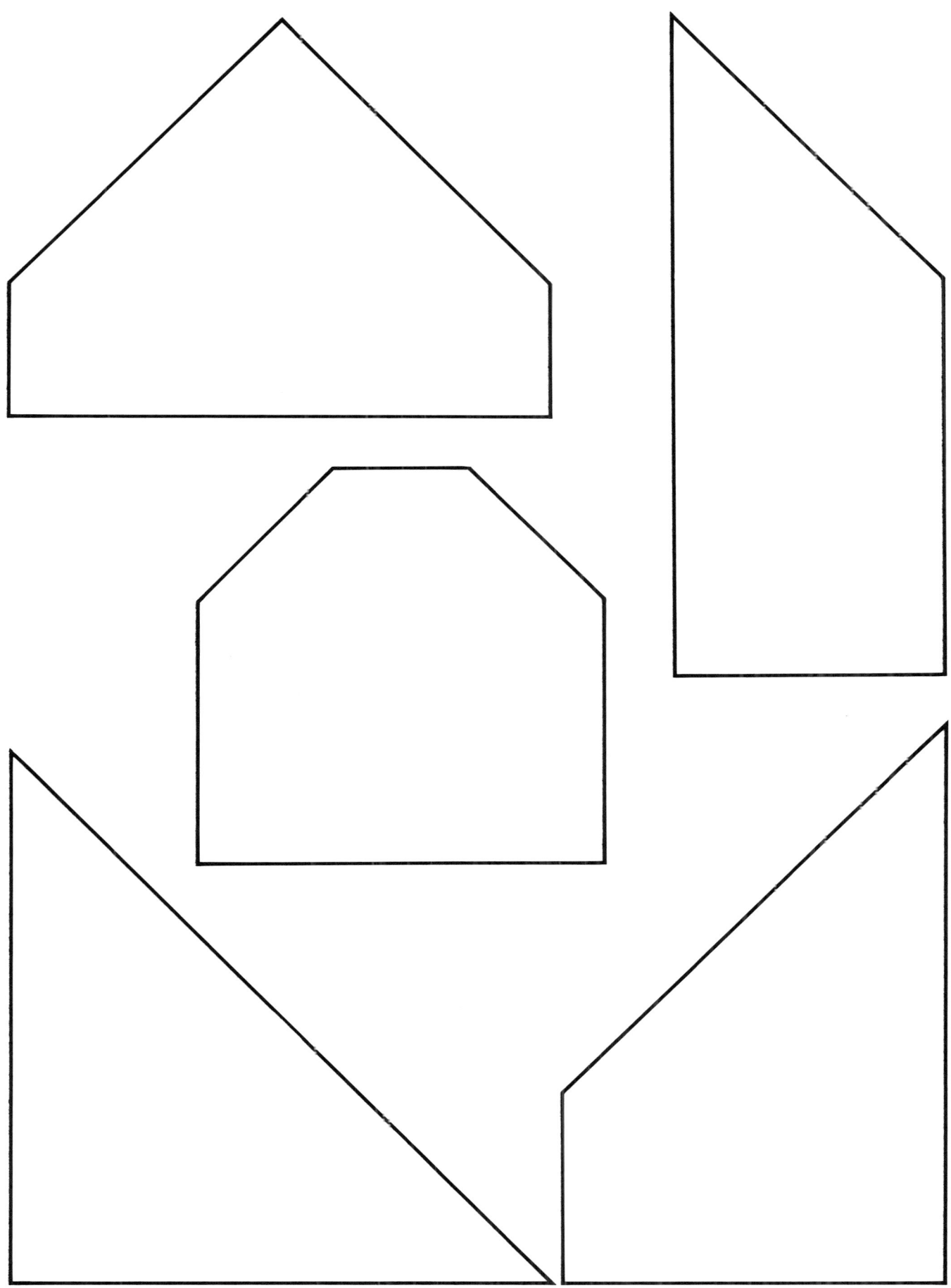

All rights reserved. Addison-Wesley Publishing Company

CONVEX POLYGONS FROM THE TANGRAM PUZZLE (continued)

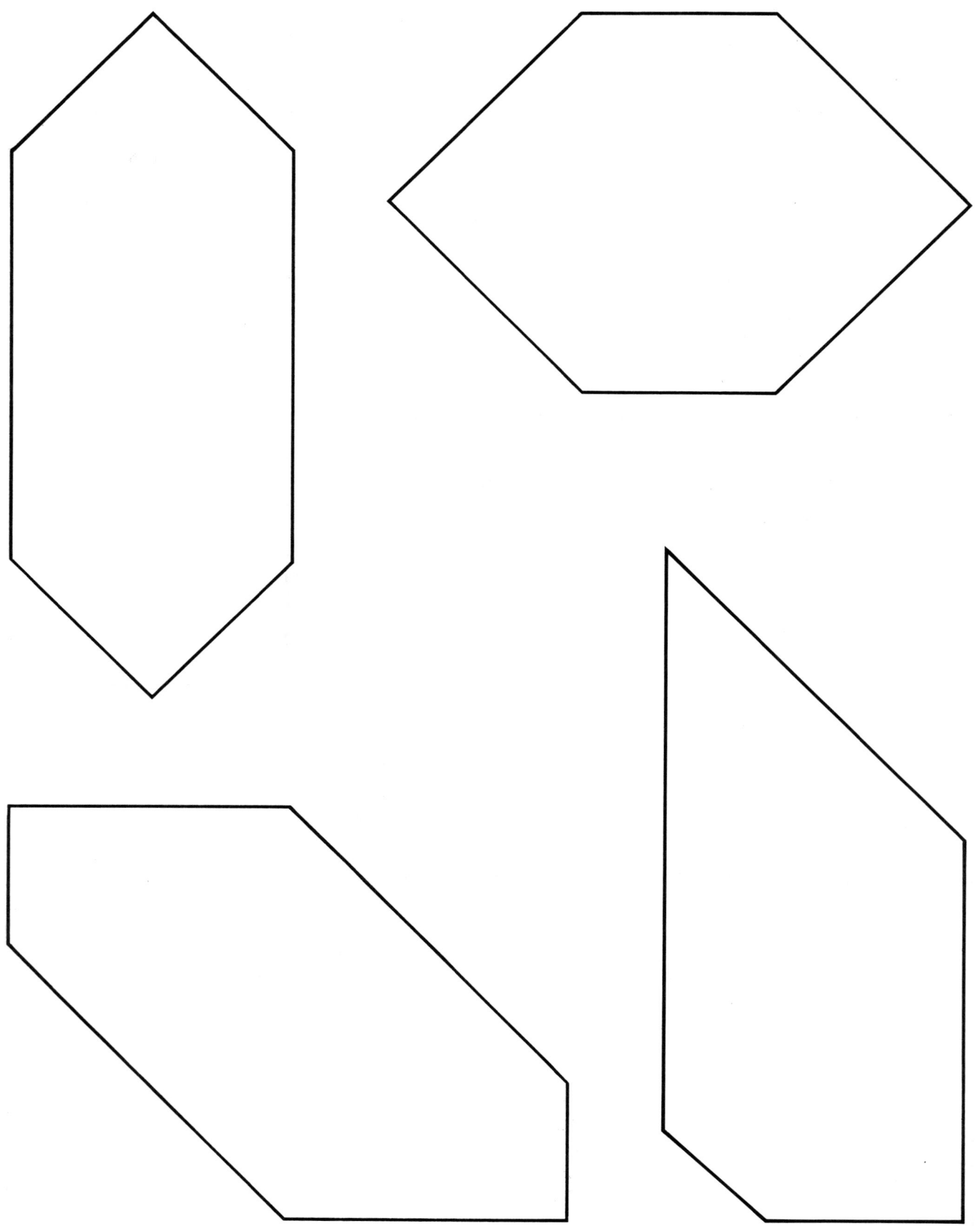

PROBLEM: If one side of the small square tangram piece has length 1, which of the 13 convex polygons above has the maximum perimeter? Find this perimeter.

7 DISSECTIONS OF A SQUARE

When cut along the broken lines, each of the shapes below yields pieces that can be rearranged to form a square. Cut out each figure and arrange the pieces in the square provided. Draw your solution in each square.

DISSECTION PUZZLES (continued)

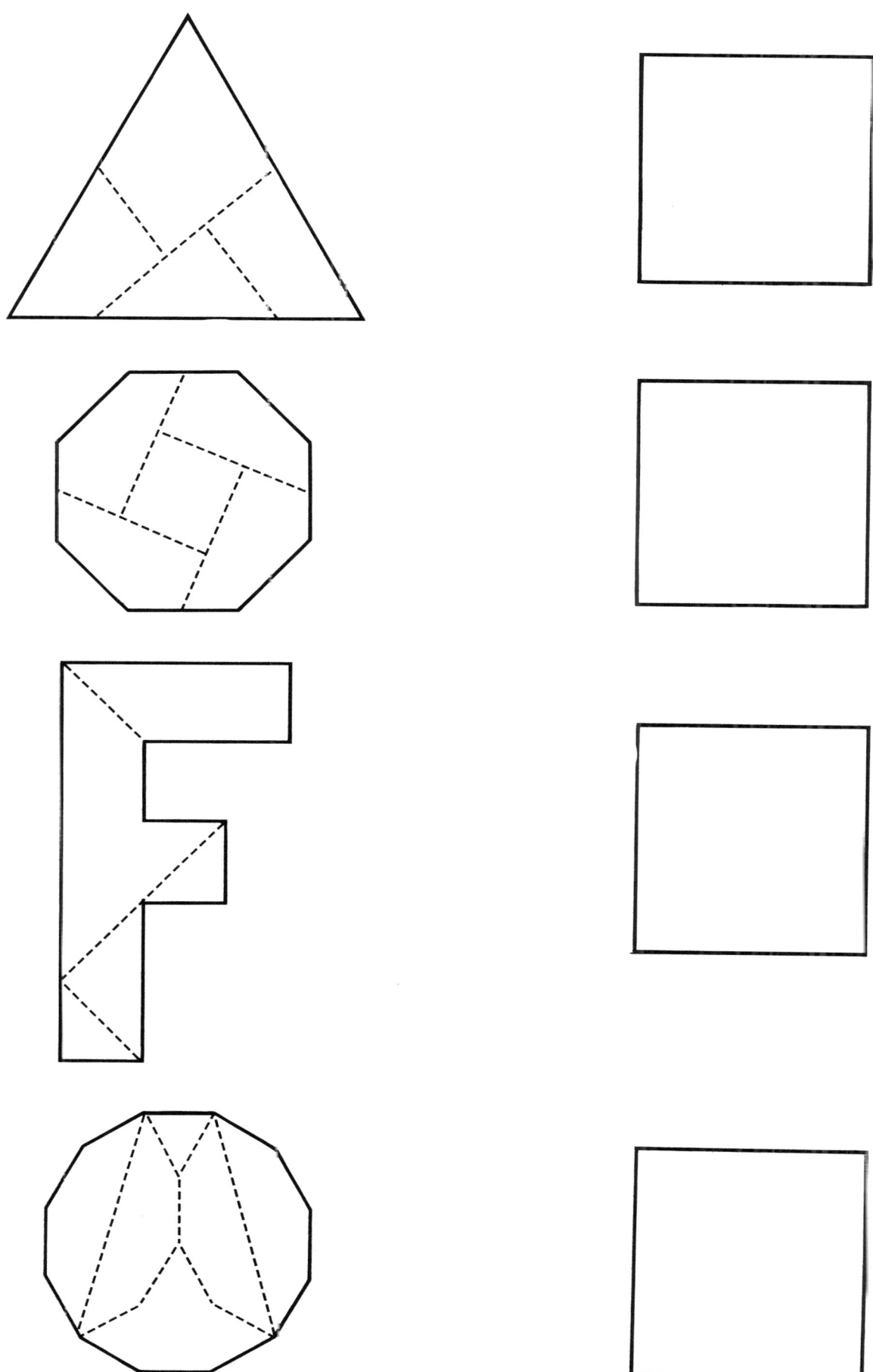

All rights reserved. Addison-Wesley Publishing Company

8 DISSECTIONS OF THE REGULAR HEXAGON AND DODECAGON

Cut out the three small hexagons and cut along all the dotted lines.
Use the 13 pieces to form the large hexagon.

Cut out the small dodecagons as indicated and use all 13 pieces to form the large dodecagon.

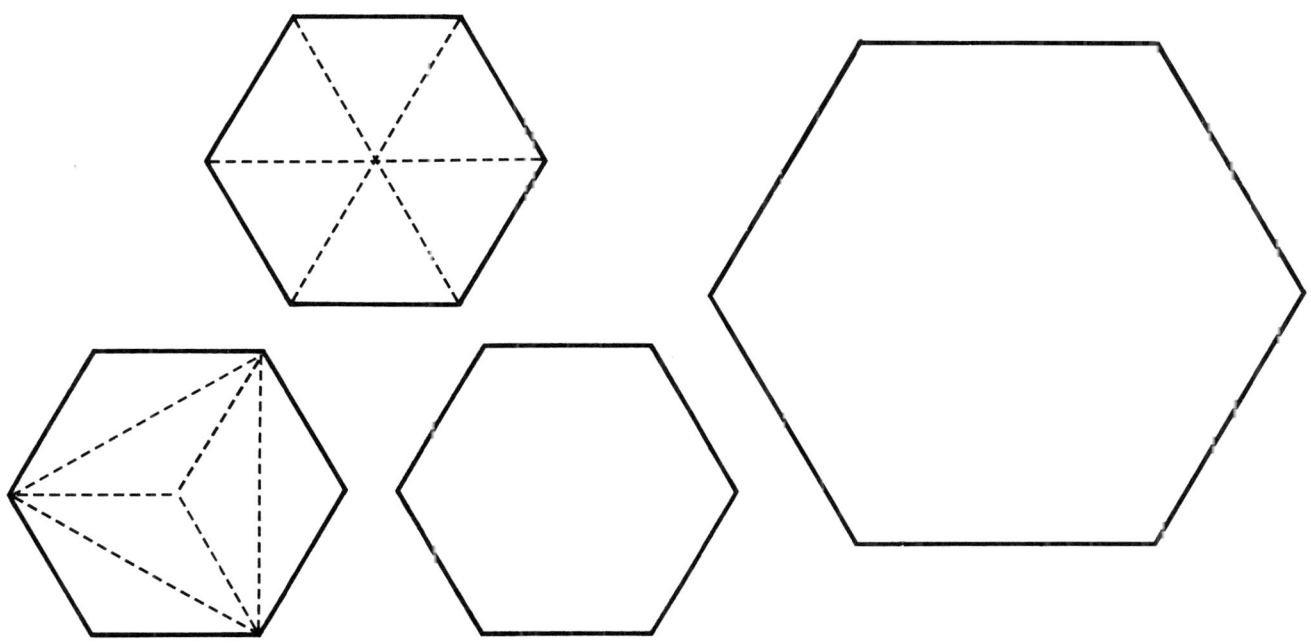

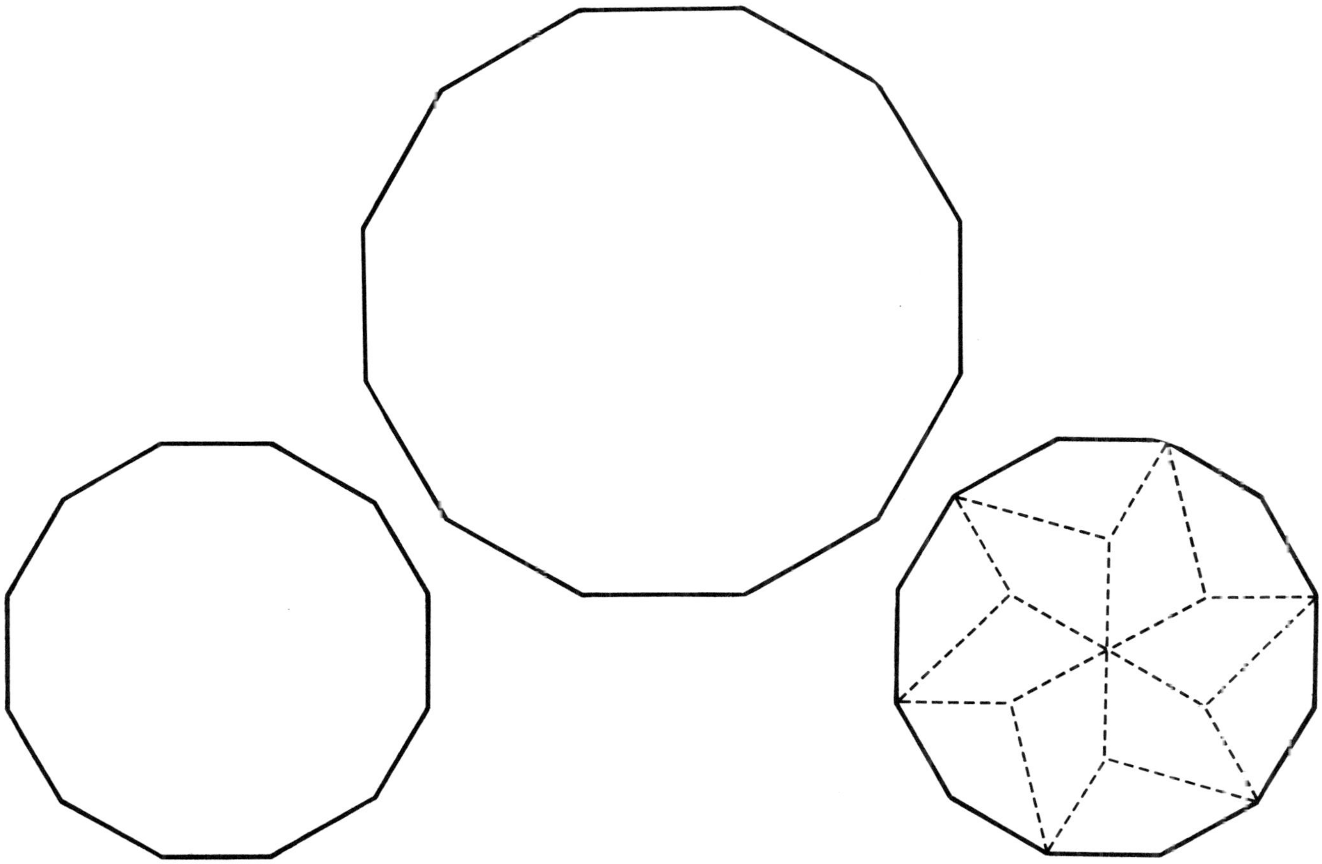

9 DISSECTIONS OF THE SIX-POINTED STAR

Cut up the three small stars along the dotted lines and fit the resulting 12 pieces together to form this large six-pointed star.

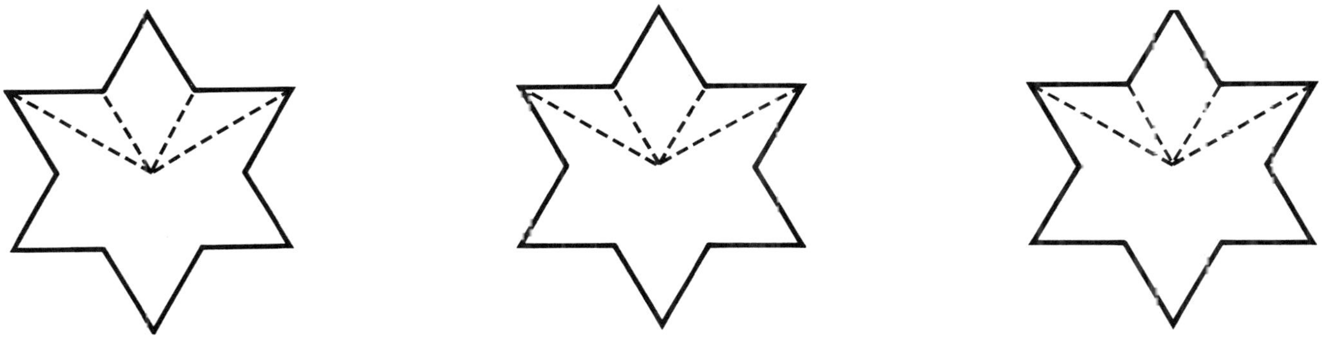

PROBLEM: How can star C be cut so that the pieces resulting from stars A, B, and C fit together to form the large six-pointed star above?

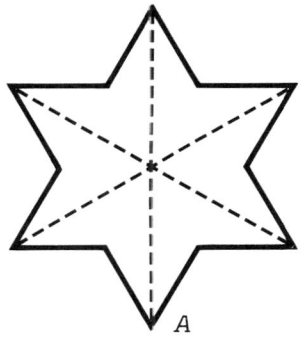
A

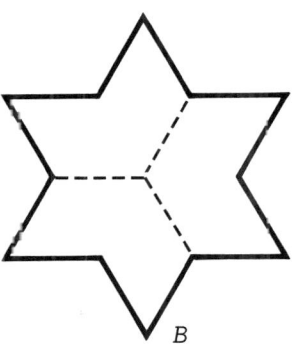
B

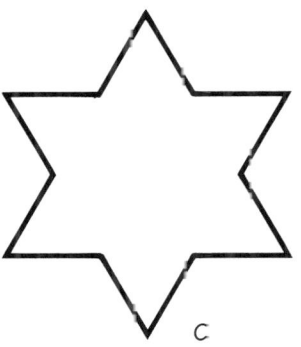
C

All rights reserved. Addison-Wesley Publishing Company

10 SEGMENTS ON GEOBOARDS

On a geoboard with *n* nails on a side (where *n* = 3, 4, 5, 6, and 7) how many different length segments are there? Draw all segments on one array. (Colored pencils may help.)

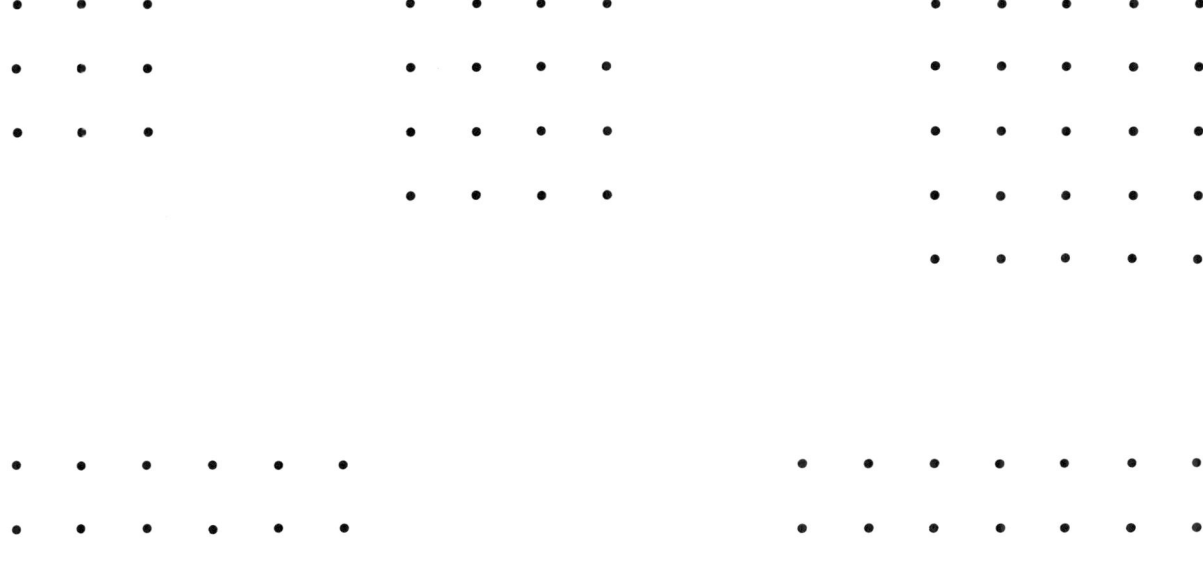

PROBLEM: Use the Pythagorean Theorem to demonstrate that there are segments (non-vertical and non-horizontal) equal in length to some horizontal segments on an *n* x *n* geoboard when $n \geq 6$.

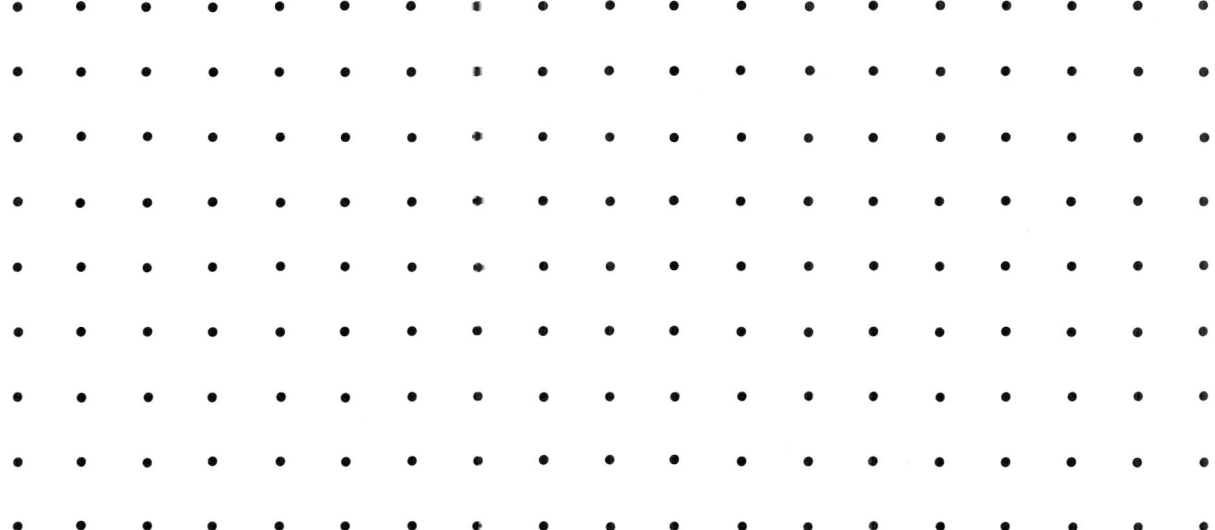

(The dot paper on the back can be used for experimenting, so the results can be recorded on the dot paper above.)

All rights reserved. Addison-Wesley Publishing Company

11 TRIANGLES AND QUADRILATERALS

On a geoboard with 3 nails on a side, how many different shaped triangles are there? How many quadrilaterals?

PROBLEM: If a small square of these dot arrays has area 1,
   how many of the triangles you found have area 1/2? How many have area 1?
   How many have area 3/2? Answer the same questions for quadrilaterals.

All rights reserved. Addison-Wesley Publishing Company

12 IRREGULAR POLYGONS ON THE GEOBOARD

It has been shown that it is possible to make a polygon with n^2 sides on an $n \times n$ geoboard, if n is greater than or equal to 7. We picture an example of a polygon with 7^2 sides on a 7×7 geoboard. Check and see if you can form a polygon with 3^2 sides on a 3×3 geoboard, 4^2 sides on a 4×4 geoboard, 5^2 sides on a 5×5 geoboard, and 6^2 sides on a 6×6 geoboard.

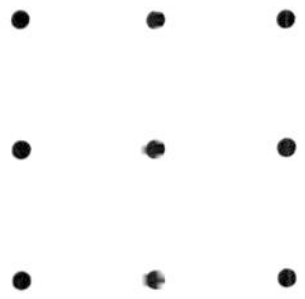

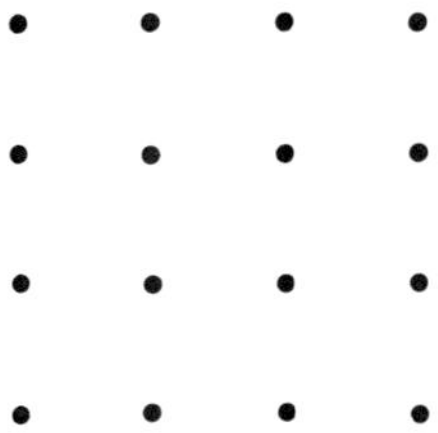

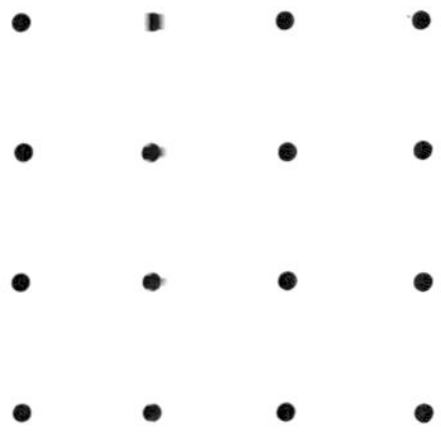

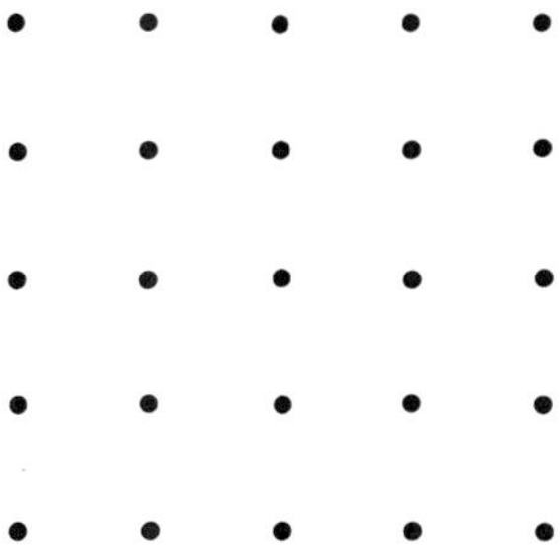

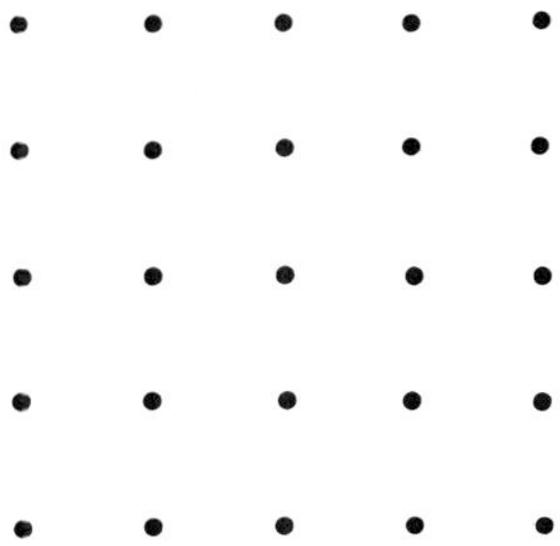

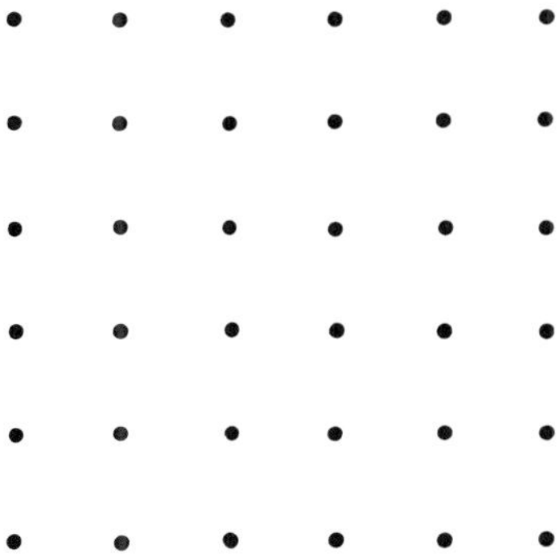

PROBLEM: We picture here a polygon with $4 \times 5 = 20$ sides constructed on a 4×5 rectangular geoboard.

How many examples can you find of a polygon with $p \times q$ sides on $p \times q$ rectangular geoboards?

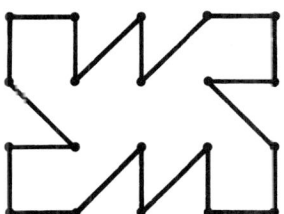

13   REGULAR POLYGONS

On circle geoboards it is possible to draw polygons of many different shapes.
If no sides cross, the polygon is called simple; otherwise it is called non-simple.

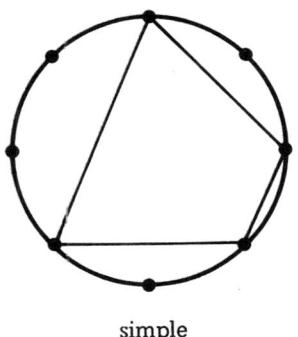

simple

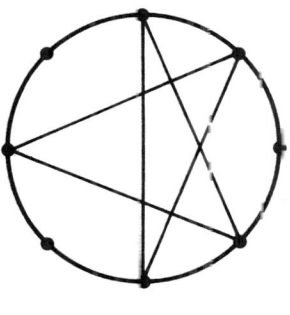

non-simple

On circle geoboards with 15, 24, 30, and 36 nails, how many simple polygons are there with all sides of equal length? Draw each one using different colored pencils.

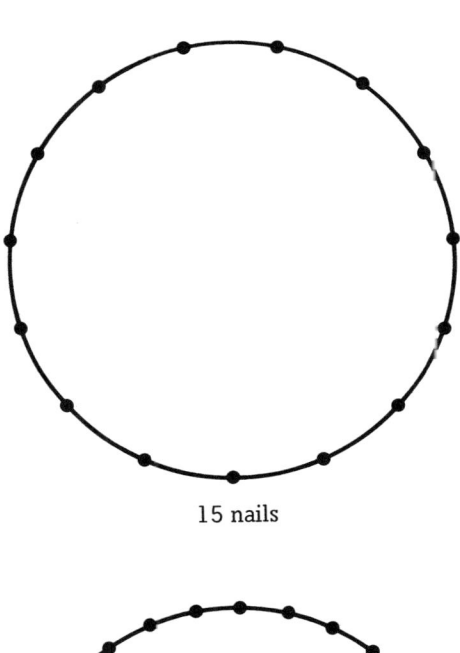

15 nails

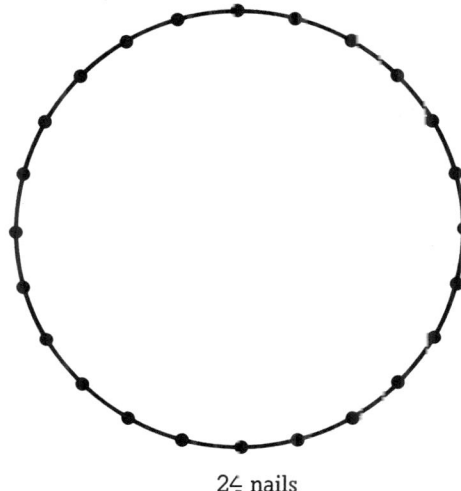

24 nails

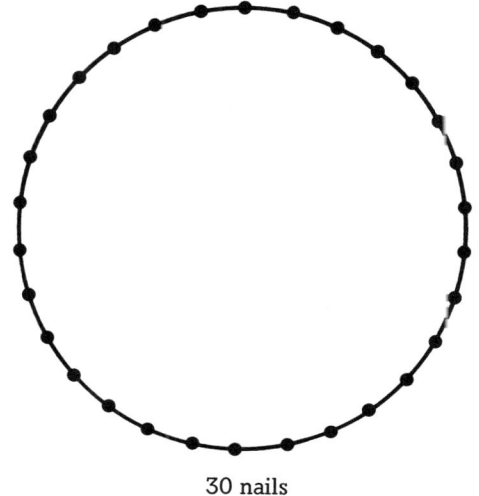

30 nails

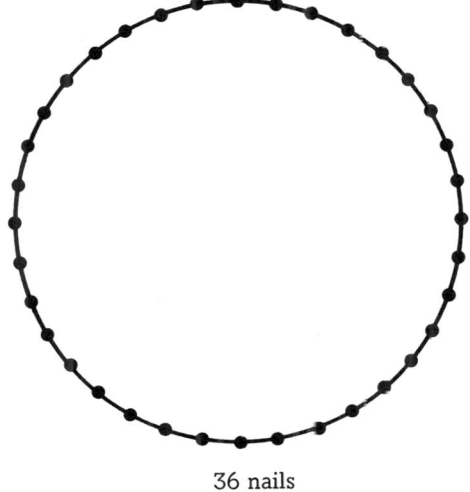

36 nails

PROBLEM: Find a simple numerical relationship between the number of nails and the number of sides for these polygons. How many simple polygons with all sides the same length exist on a circle geoboard with 60 nails?

All rights reserved. Addison-Wesley Publishing Company

14 STAR POLYGONS

Begin with evenly spaced points on a circle. Draw a polygon by joining every second point, or every third, or every fourth, etc. If this polygon is a non-simple polygon, it is called a star polygon.

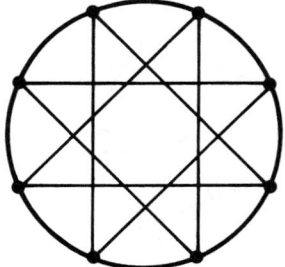

a star polygon
made by starting
with 8 points and
joining every third
point

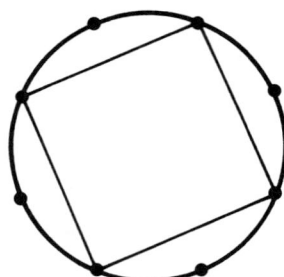

not a star
polygon

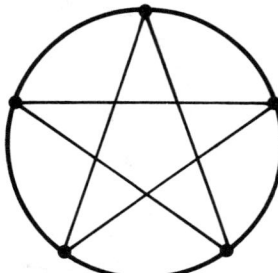

a star polygon
made by starting
with 5 points and
joining every second
point

Four star polygons can be drawn on a circular geoboard with 18 nails.
Draw each of them on the dot paper below. (Colored pencils are recommended.)

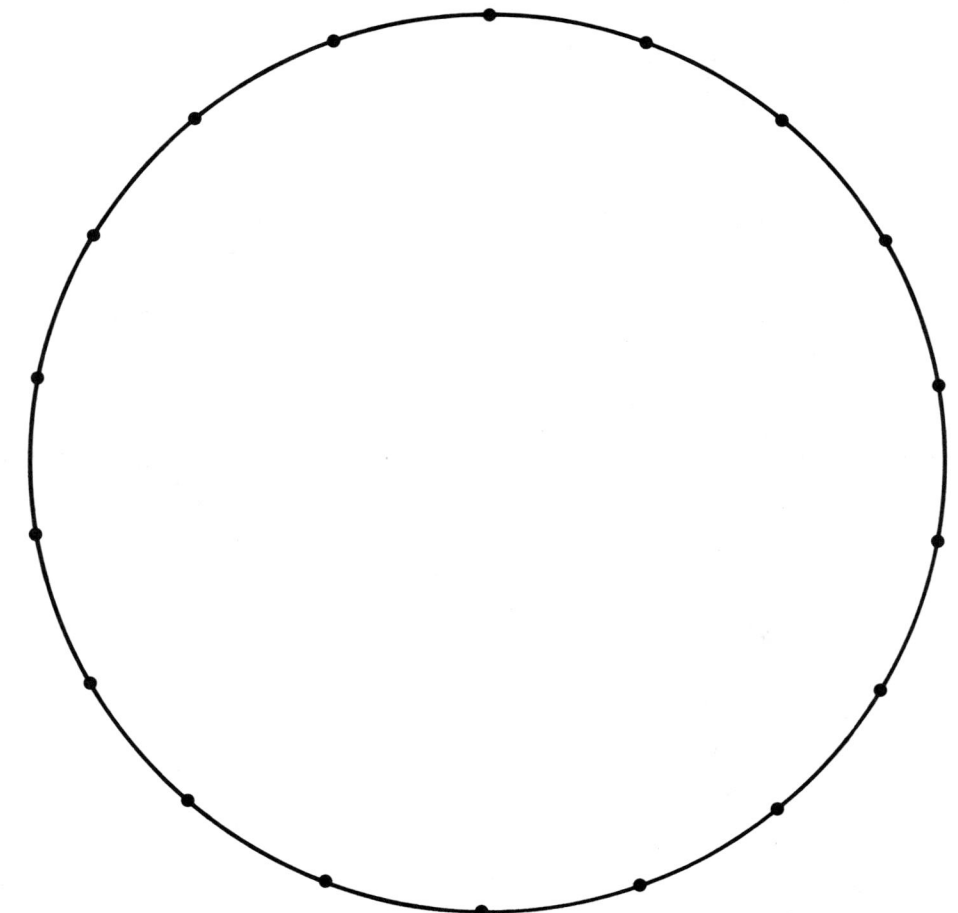

PROBLEM: A star polygon which has been drawn from n evenly spaced points by joining each pth point is called the star polygon $\{{n \atop p}\}$. The example at the top left of the page is the star polygon $\{{8 \atop 3}\}$. Name each of the star polygons that you drew in the investigation.

15 STAR POLYGONS

Five star polygons can be drawn on a circular geoboard with 24 nails.
Draw each of them on the dot paper below. (Colored pencils are recommended.)

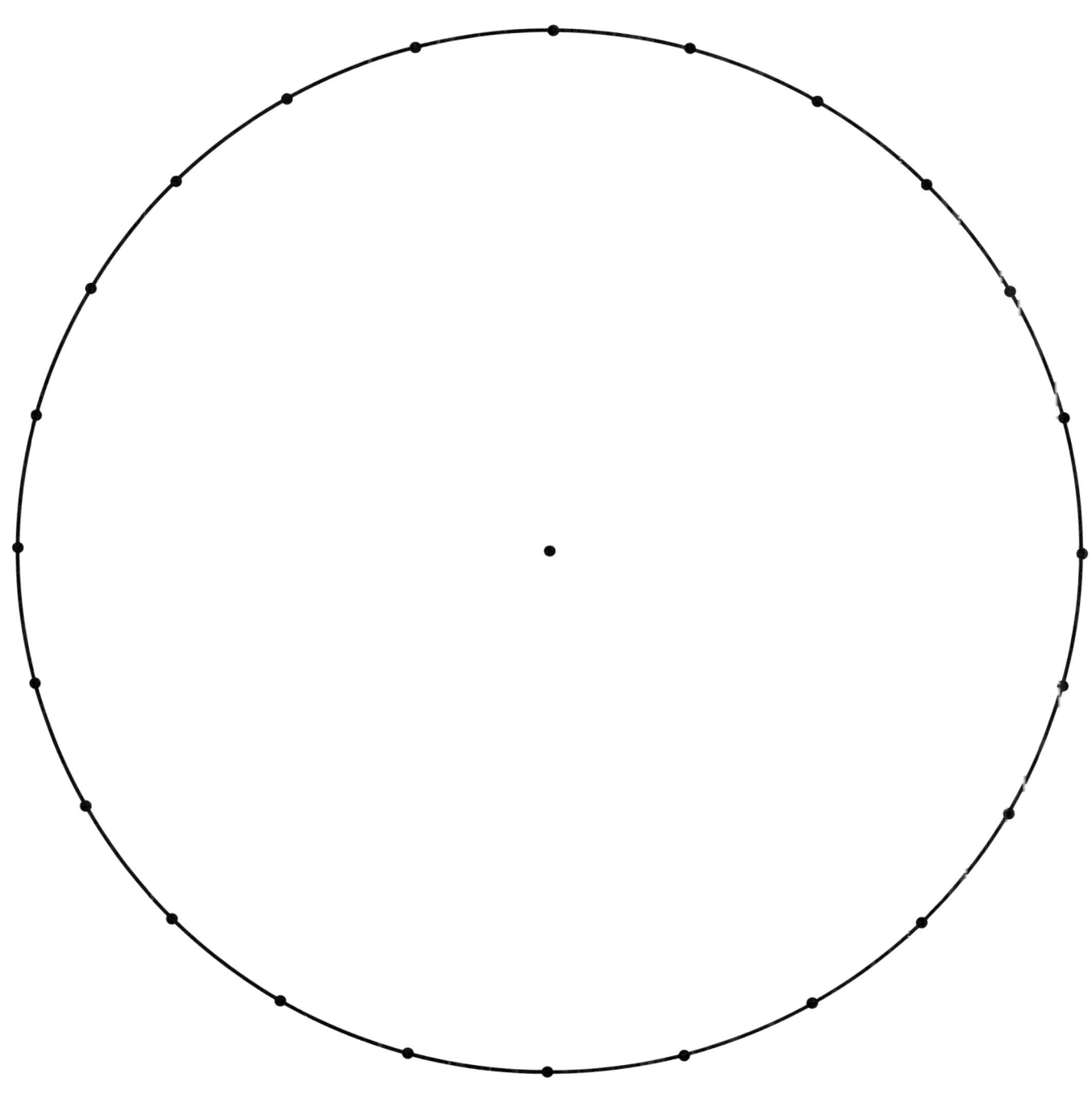

PROBLEM: Find a formula for the number of degrees in each vertex angle of the star polygon $\left\{ \begin{matrix} n \\ p \end{matrix} \right\}$.

All rights reserved. Addison-Wesley Publishing Company

16 PENTOMINOES

A pentominoe is a polygon which bounds 5 squares, each square touching another square along an edge.

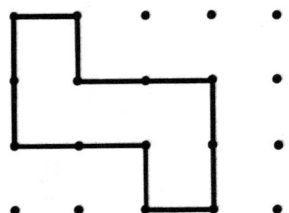

This is a pentominoe.

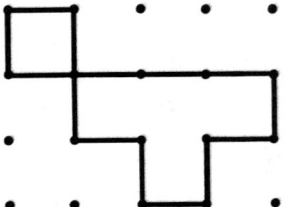

This is not a pentominoe.

Draw each of the 12 different shaped pentominoes. (Recall that two pentominoes are of the same shape if one can be made to coincide with the other by sliding, turning or flipping.)

PROBLEM: Find a way to place all 12 pentominoes on an 8 x 8 checkerboard.
Find a way to place 6 pentominoes on an 8 x 8 checkerboard so that none of the remaining 6 pentominoes will fit on the board without an overlap.

17 SYMMETRY OF THE PENTOMINOES

one half folds exactly
onto the other half

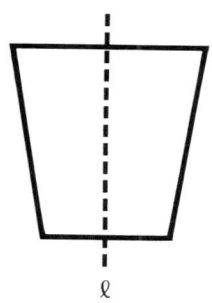

ℓ is a line of symmetry

turn 180° about point C to move
the figure onto itself

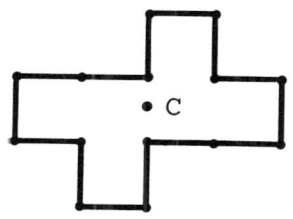

C is a center of rotational
symmetry

not possible to fold
one half exactly onto the
other half.
Only a 360° turn
moves the figure onto itself.

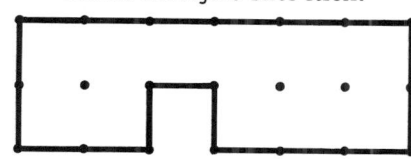

no line of symmetry
no center of rotational symmetry

Draw each pentominoe and sketch all lines of symmetry and all centers of rotational symmetry.

PROBLEM: There are many ways to put three pentominoes together to form
a 3 x 5 rectangle. Show that in all of these ways there must be at least one
pentominoe with no symmetry. (Hint: Use only the pentominoes possessing symmetry
and show by exhaustion that a 3 x 5 rectangle cannot be formed with them.)

All rights reserved. Addison-Wesley Publishing Company

18 SYMMETRY PATTERNS

In each of the following circular regions below, complete the design so that it satisfies the symmetry condition specified (and no others).

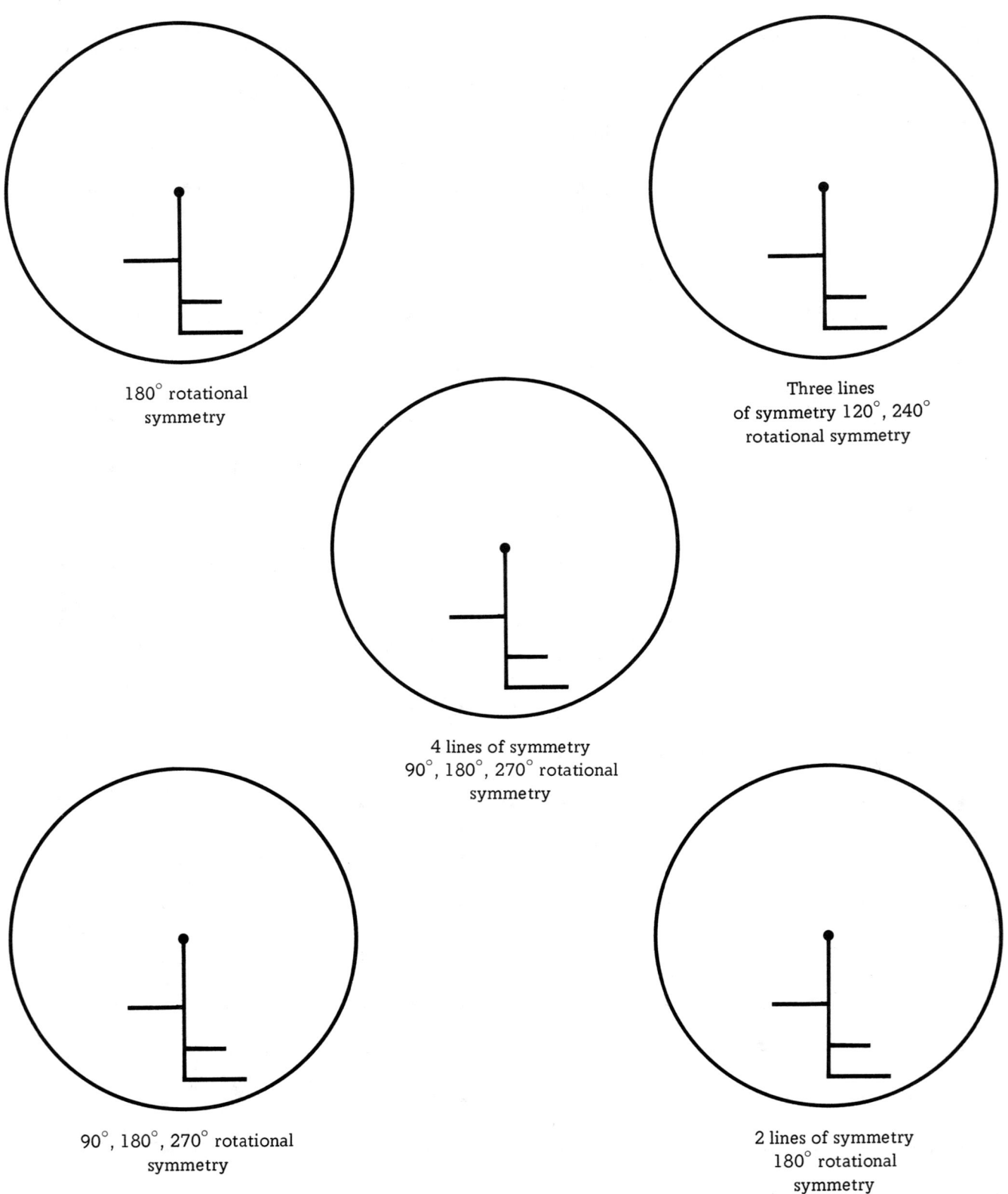

180° rotational symmetry

Three lines of symmetry 120°, 240° rotational symmetry

4 lines of symmetry 90°, 180°, 270° rotational symmetry

90°, 180°, 270° rotational symmetry

2 lines of symmetry 180° rotational symmetry

PROBLEM: A triangle has either three lines of symmetry, one line of symmetry, or zero lines of symmetry. What are the possible number of lines of symmetry for pentagons and hexagons?

19 SYMMETRY PATTERNS

Using only a compass, duplicate this design. Use a colored pencil and draw in all lines of symmetry. Describe the rotational symmetry.

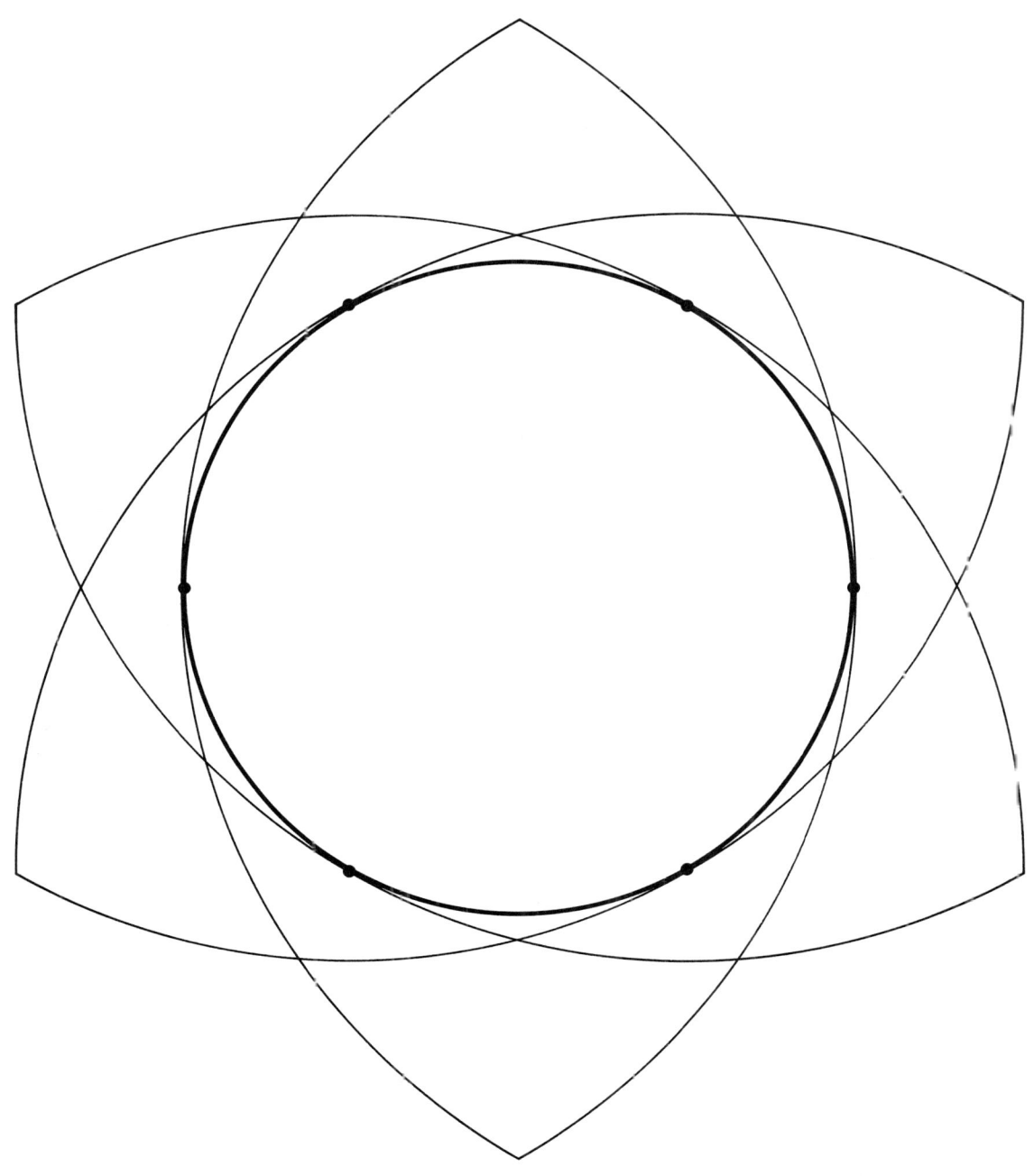

PROBLEM: How can you add to the design (using only a compass) so that the new design has only one line of symmetry?

20 ROTATIONAL SYMMETRY ON A GEOBOARD

Pictured is a figure with 90° rotational symmetry on a 5 x 5 geoboard. The figure is constructed by drawing four identical paths which satisfy these conditions.

1. All paths begin at the center nail and move from nail to nail until reaching an outside boundary nail.
2. None of the four paths touch or cross each other or themselves.
3. Once a path reaches an outside boundary it stops.

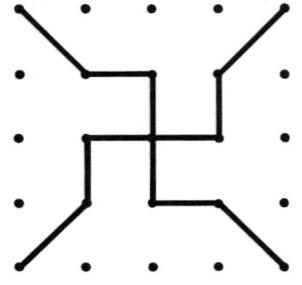

There are 24 figures with 90° rotational symmetry that can be drawn satisfying all of the above conditions. Draw them.

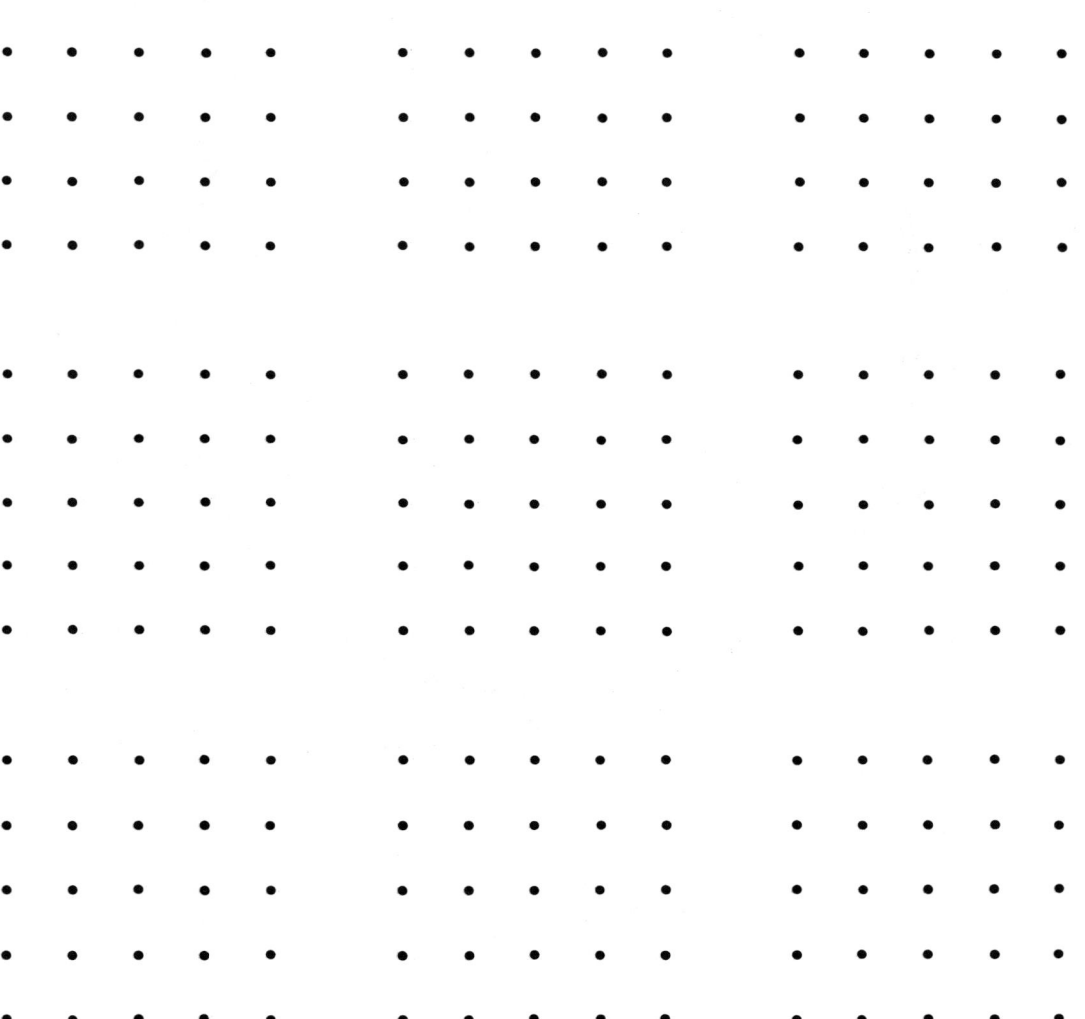

21 HEXOMINOES

A hexominoe is a polygon which bounds six squares, each square touching another square along an edge.

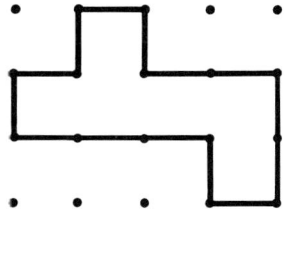

a hexominoe

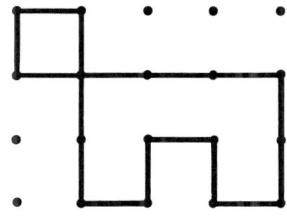

not a hexominoe

Draw the 35 different shaped hexominoes. If the squares of the hexominoes are colored alternately black and white, how many of them will have three black and three white squares, and how many of them will have four squares of one color and two of the other color?

PROBLEM: Which ones of the 35 hexominoes can be folded along edges to form a cube?

All rights reserved. Addison-Wesley Publishing Company

22 HEXIAMONDS

A hexiamond is a polygon which bounds six equilateral triangles, each triangle touching another triangle along an edge.

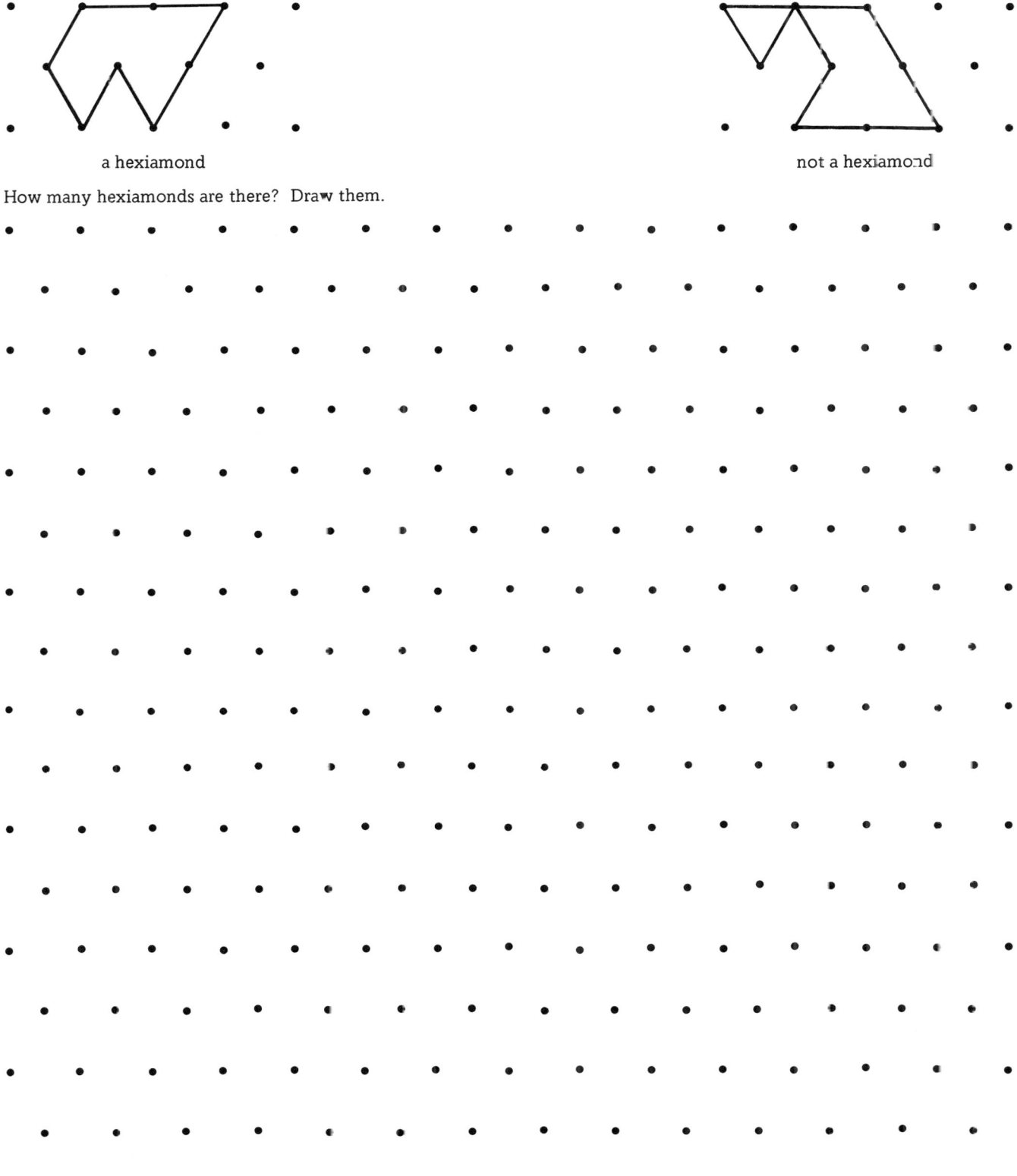

a hexiamond

not a hexiamond

How many hexiamonds are there? Draw them.

PROBLEM: Cut out all 12 hexiamonds and show that they can be arranged to form a rhombus with sides six units long.

All rights reserved. Addison-Wesley Publishing Company

23 A THEOREM FOR QUADRILATERALS

Join the midpoints of adjacent sides for these quadrilaterals.
What type of figure do you obtain?

PROBLEM: From the situation above, conjecture a theorem about quadrilaterals. Can you prove your conjecture? Recall that the segment joining the midpoints of two sides of a triangle is parallel to the third side and half as long.

24 ANGLE TRISECTORS OF A TRIANGLE

For each of the triangles below use a protractor to trisect each of the angles.
Let X, Y, Z be the points of intersection of the adjacent trisectors.
The points X, Y, and Z are the vertices of what type of triangle?
Conjecture a theorem.

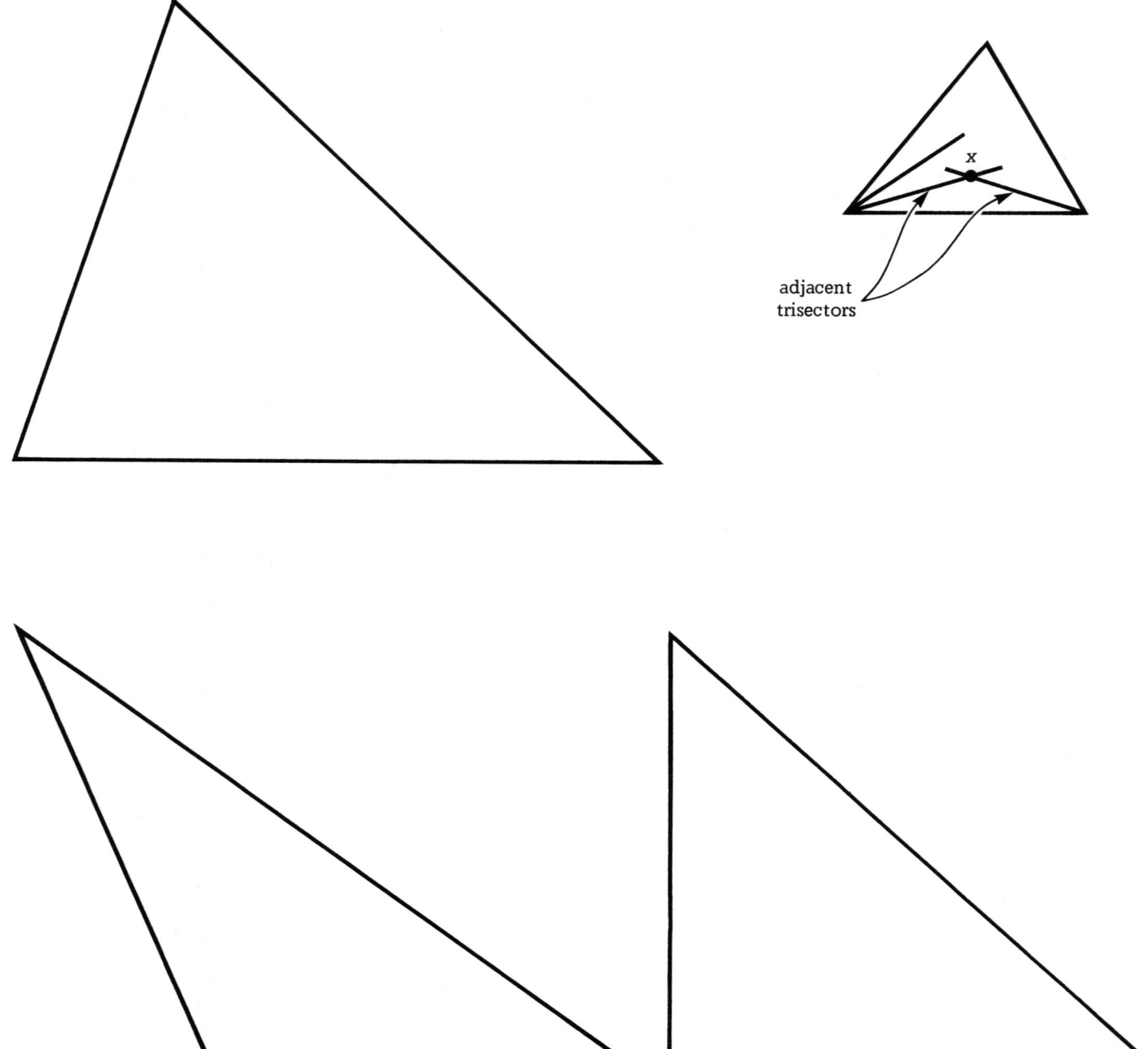

PROBLEM: In the above constructions draw the segment from X to the third vertex of the original triangle. Similarly, draw segments from the points Y and Z. Are these three segments concurrent?

25   THREE SPECIAL POINTS OF A TRIANGLE

1. Join each vertex to the midpoint of the opposite side.
2. Construct each of the three altitudes (perpendiculars to each side and through the opposite vertex).
3. Construct the perpendicular bisectors of each side.

Do this for each of the triangles given. These constructions yield three points called the centroid, the orthocenter, and the circumcenter. What theorem do you conjecture about these three points?

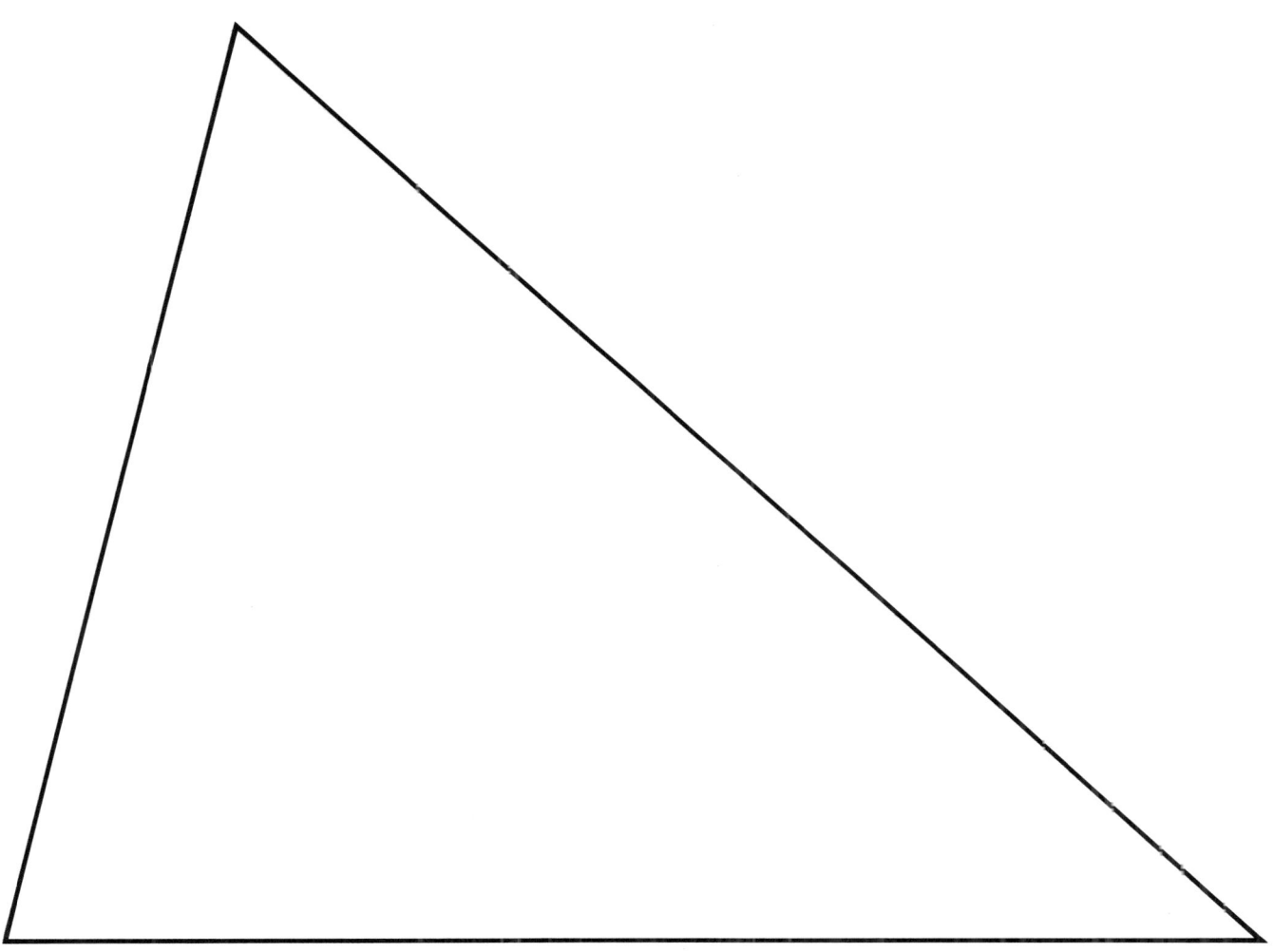

25 THREE SPECIAL POINTS OF A TRIANGLE (continued)

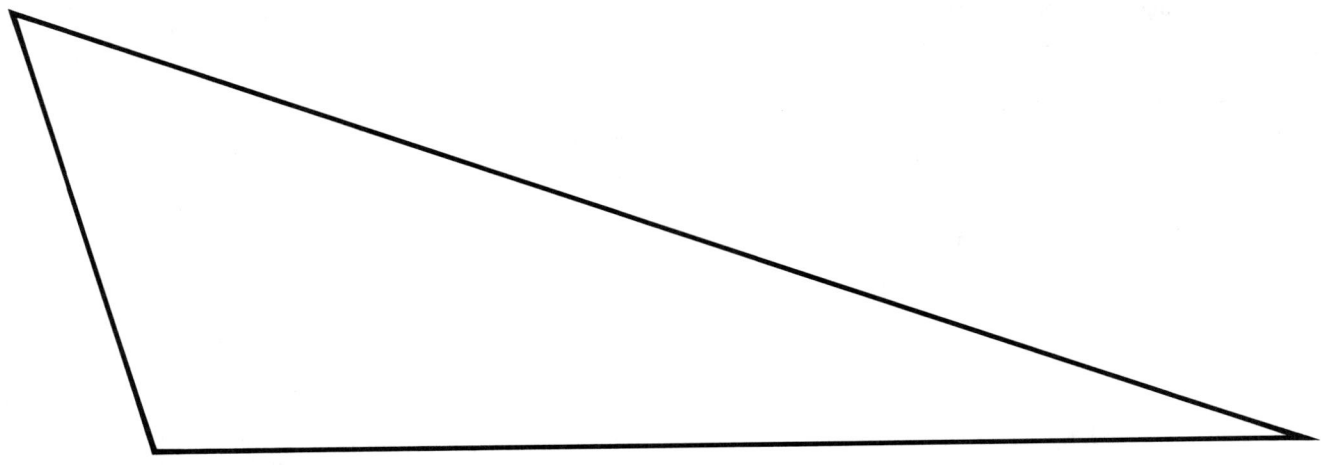

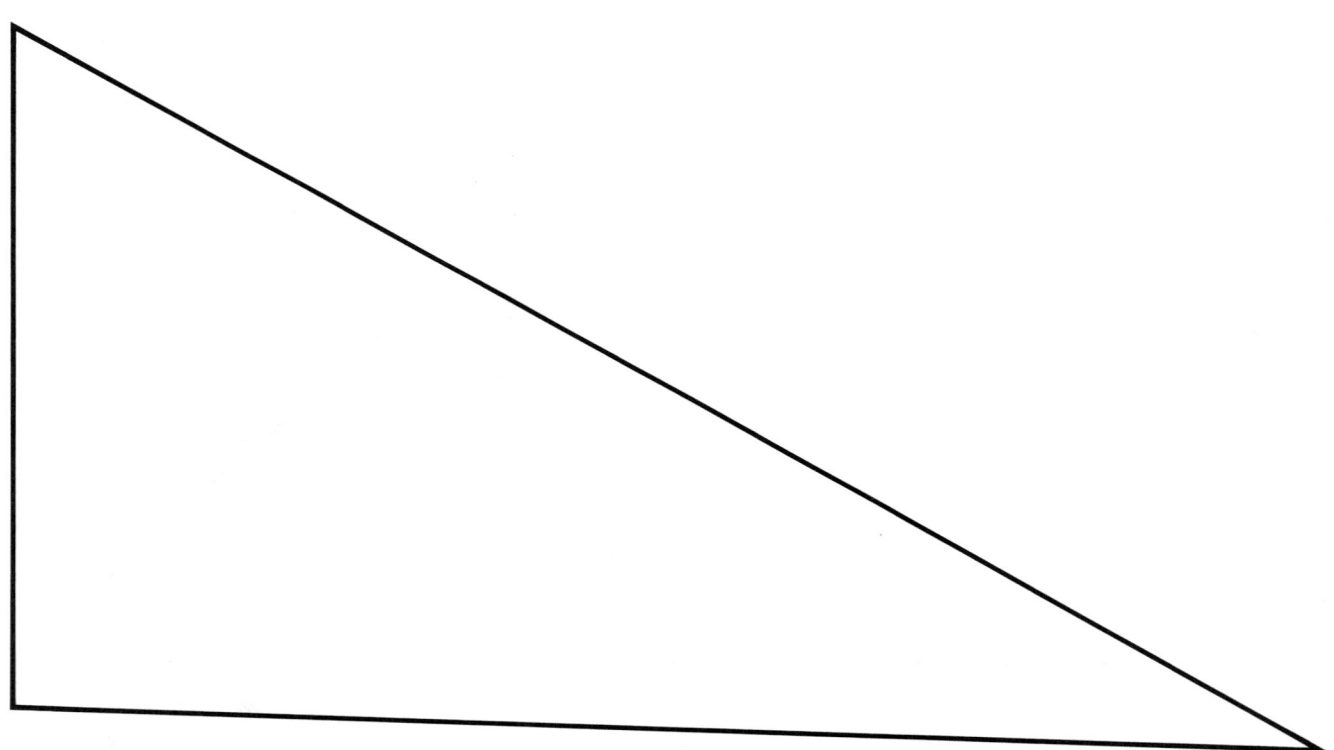

PROBLEM: In the first part of this investigation we obtained three points.
(These three points are called the centroid, orthocenter, and circumcenter.)
Use a centimeter ruler and measure the distances between these three points.
Is the distance from the circumcenter to the orthocenter
always three times the distance from the circumcenter to the centroid?

26   NINE INTERESTING POINTS

Use a Mira or compass and straight edge to construct the following nine points in the triangle below:

   a.   the midpoints of the three sides
   b.   the feet of the three altitudes
   c.   the midpoints of the segments from the three vertices to the orthocenter. (The orthocenter is the point of intersection of the three altitudes.)

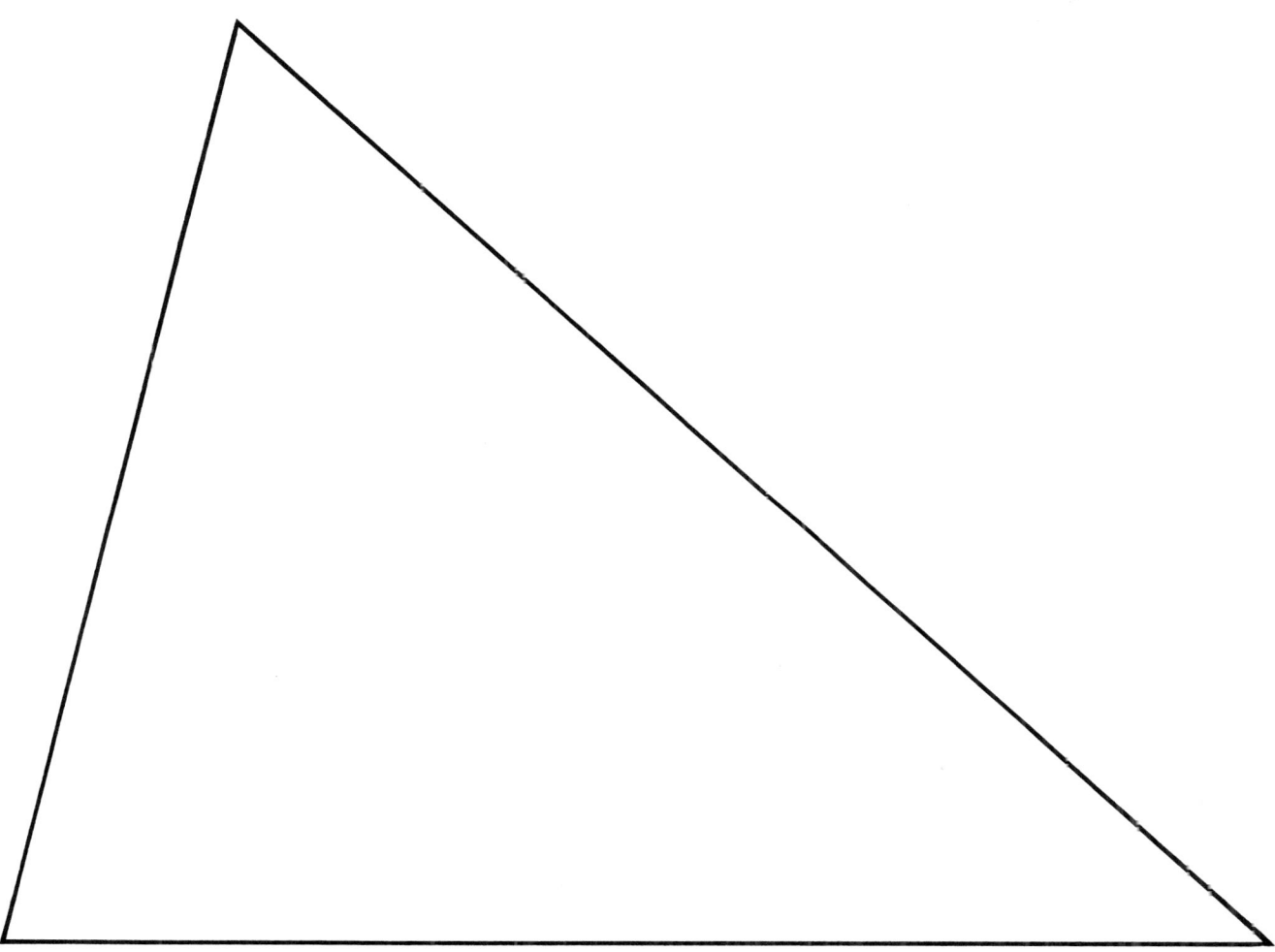

There is a unique circle through any three non-collinear points. Select three of the above nine points and construct the circle through them. How are the remaining six points related to this circle? Does your discovery seem to be true for all triangles?

PROBLEM: How is the center of the circle you constructed above related to the line (the Euler line) containing the centroid, the circumcenter, and the orthocenter?

27 A THEOREM FOR TRIANGLES

For each of the triangles below construct equilateral triangles externally on each side, and join the centroids of these three triangles. What do you discover?

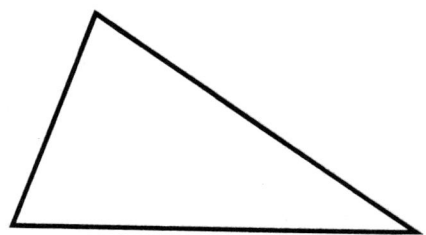

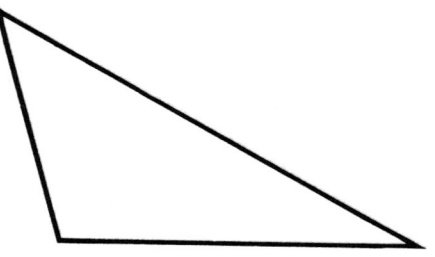

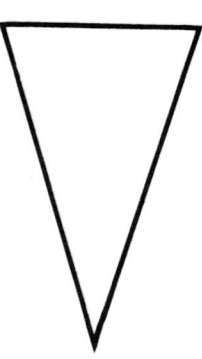

PROBLEM: Use a centimeter ruler and measure to find the area of the triangle constructed on the longest side and the area of the triangle whose vertices are the three centroids. Which triangle has the largest area? Is there consistency in this comparison?

28 A THEOREM FOR TRIANGLES

For each of the equilateral triangles below construct the perpendicular segments from X to each side of the triangle. How does the length of the altitude of the triangle compare with the length of these three segments? Conjecture a theorem.

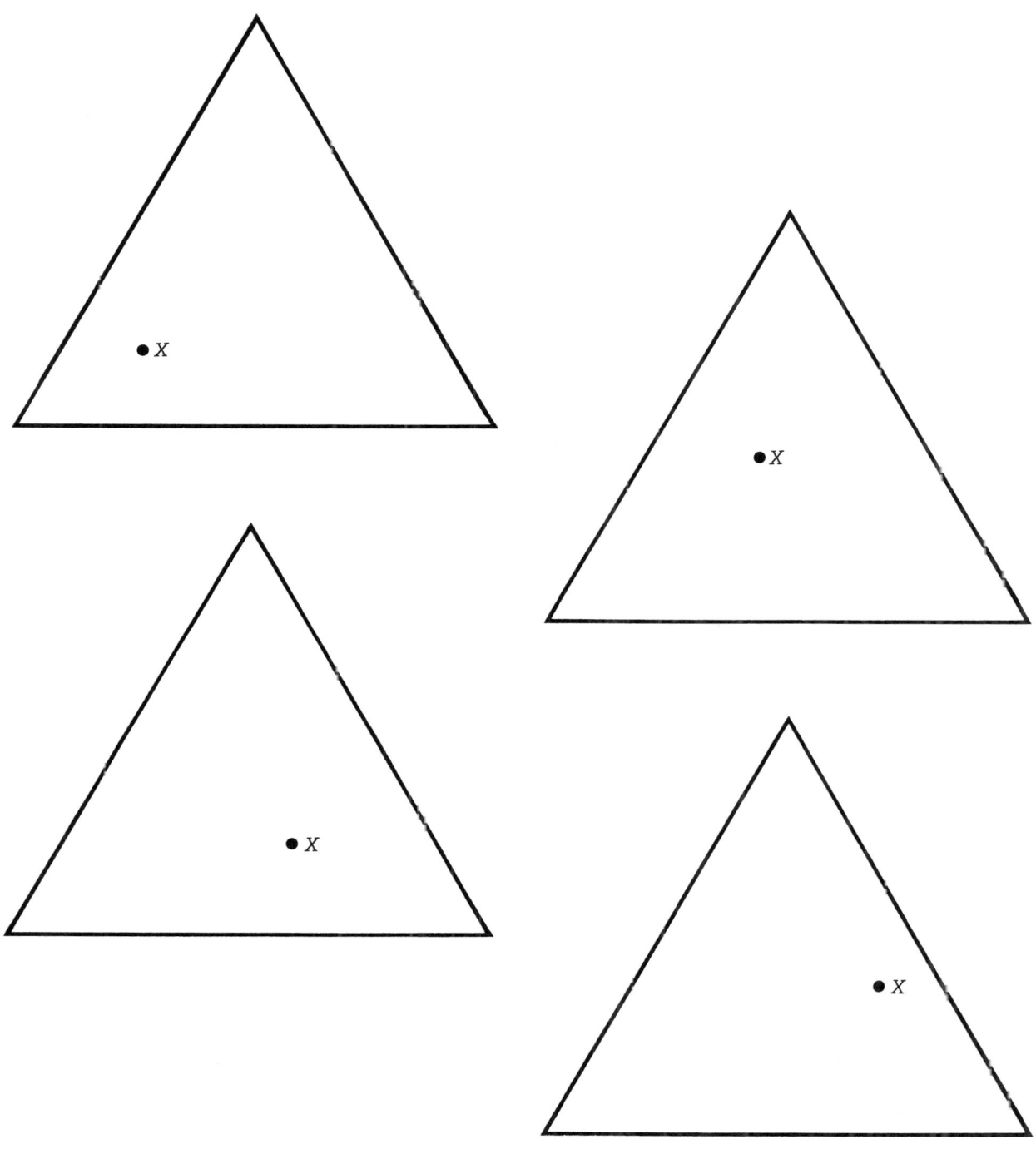

PROBLEM: Prove your conjecture. (Hint: Use the fact that the area of the equilateral triangle is equal to the sum of the areas of its pieces.)

29 A THEOREM FOR PARALLELOGRAMS

For each parallelogram below construct squares externally on the sides. Join the centroids (centers) of the four squares. What theorem do you conjecture about the quadrilateral constructed in this way?

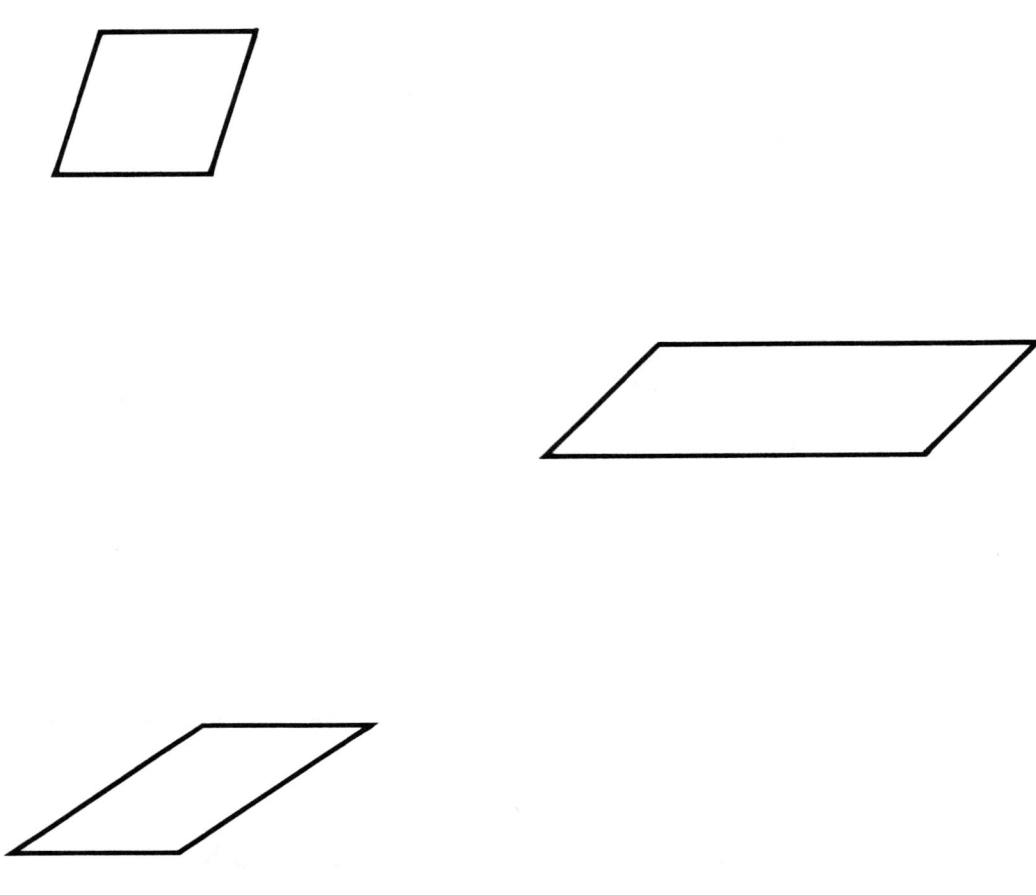

PROBLEM: Begin with two parallelograms with corresponding sides the same length, for which the acute angles do *not* have the same measure.

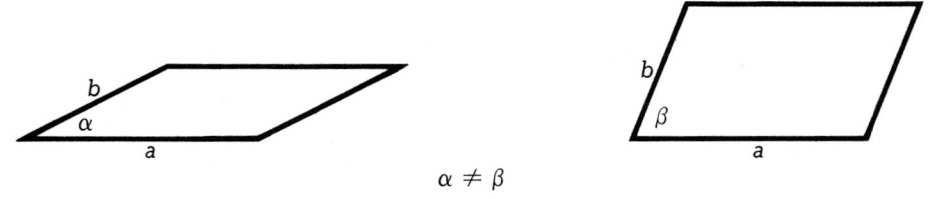

$\alpha \neq \beta$

For each parallelogram construct a quadrilateral as outlined in the investigation above. Do the two quadrilaterals have the same shape? The same area?

30 TESSELLATIONS WITH REGULAR POLYGONS

A polygon tessellates the plane if multiple copies of it can be arranged to cover the plane with no overlapping and no gaps. For example, squares tessellate the plane.

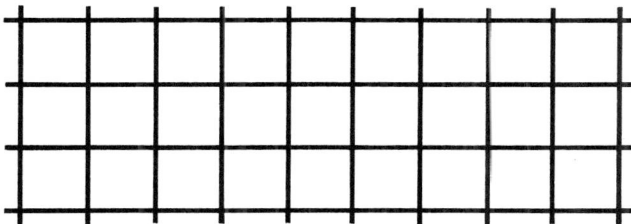

Use the regular polygons below as templates and cut out 12 copies of each. Experiment with arrangements of these polygons. Which ones tessellate the plane?

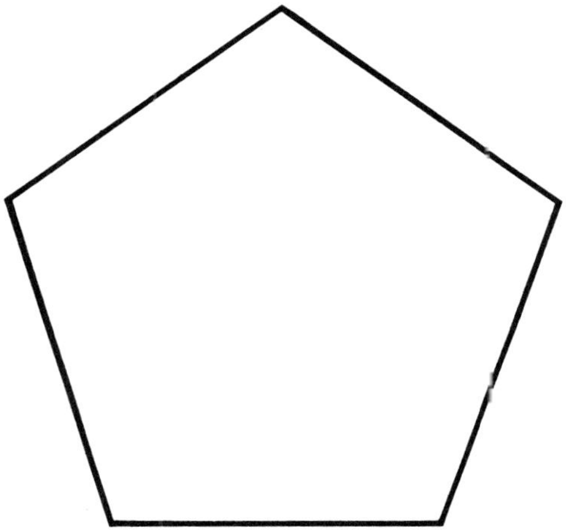

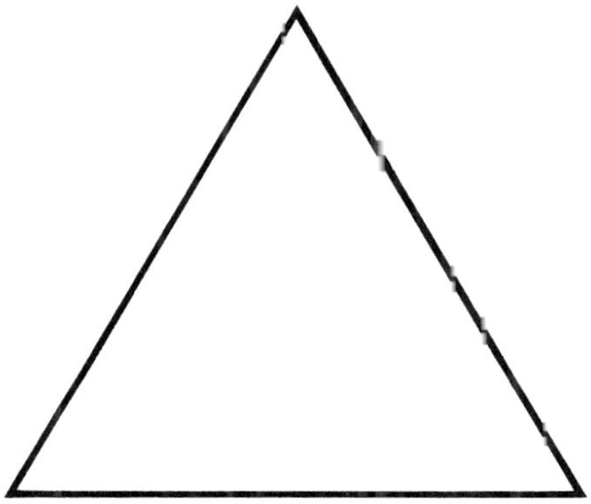

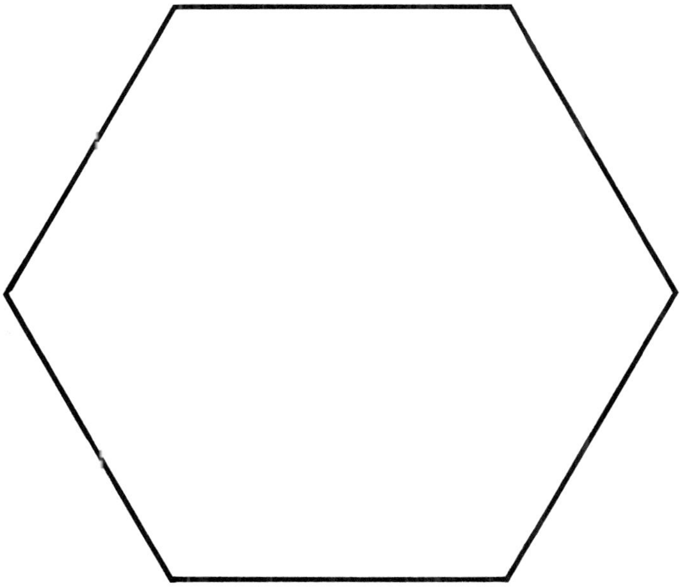

PROBLEM: What is the measure of the vertex angle for regular 3-gons, 4-gons, 5-gons, 6-gons, n-gons? How is the size of the vertex angle related to whether or not the polygon tessellates the plane?

All rights reserved. Addison-Wesley Publishing Company

31 TESSELLATIONS OF TRIANGLES AND QUADRILATERALS

Use these triangles and quadrilaterals as templates and cut out 12 copies of each. Experiement. Which of these triangles and quadrilaterals tessellate the plane?

PROBLEM: The sum of the measures of the angles of a triangle is _____ .

The sum of the measures of the angles of a quadrilateral is _____ .
Illustrate these facts by showing that six copies of any of these triangles or four copies of any of these quadrilaterals can be arranged to completely surround a point. Can these arrangements be extended to form a tessellation?

All rights reserved. Addison-Wesley Publishing Company

32 TESSELLATIONS OF TRIANGLES AND QUADRILATERALS

Draw a tessellation using this triangle so that all vertices are surrounded alike.

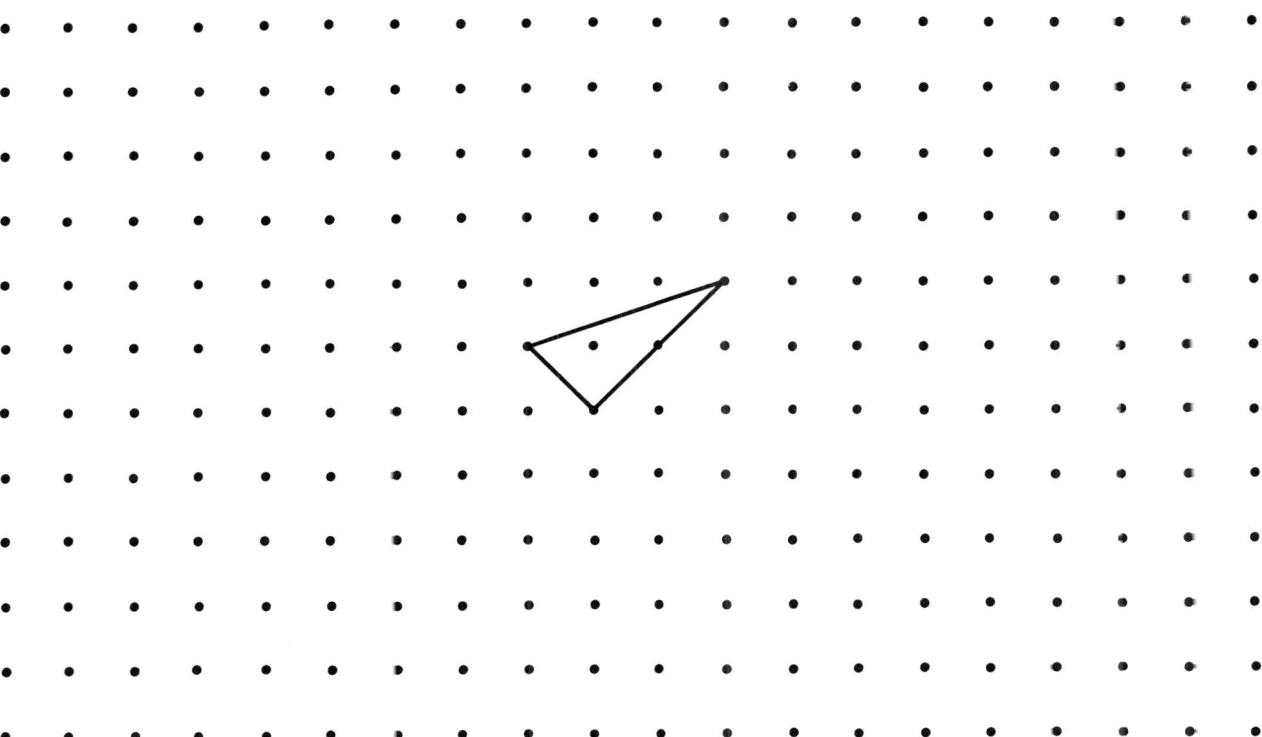

Draw a tessellation using this quadrilateral so that all vertices are surrounded alike.

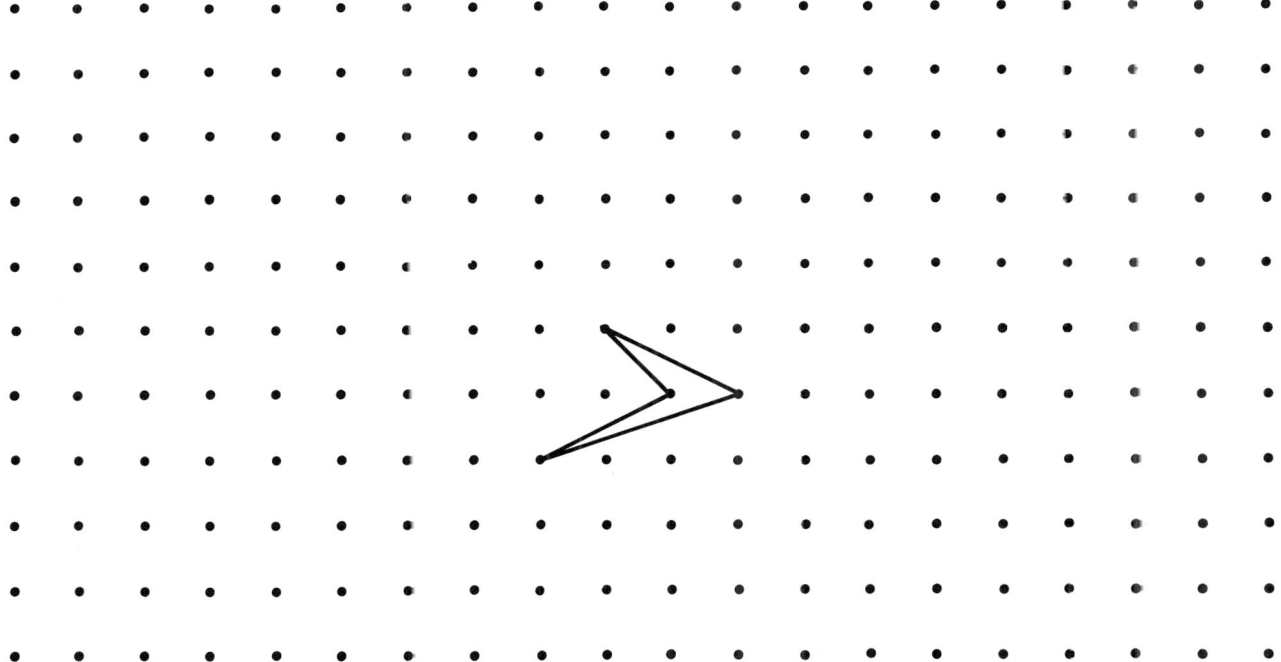

PROBLEM: On the isometric dot paper on the back of this page draw a tessellation of the trapezoid shape in which there are at least two types of vertices. Some look like

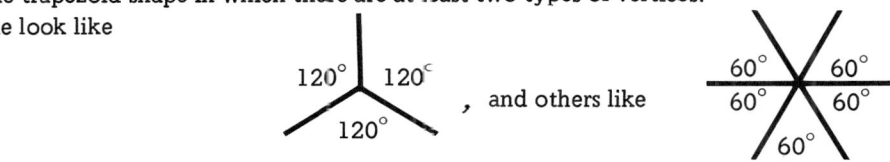

, and others like

All rights reserved. Addison-Wesley Publishing Company

33 TESSELLATIONS OF PENTOMINOES

Draw, if possible, tessellations of each of the pentominoes given here.

PROBLEM: Select one of the three pentominoes above. Can you find a tessellation with a different pattern from the one you found while completing this investigation? Color the tessellation in an interesting way.

33 TESSELLATIONS OF PENTOMINOES (continued)

34 TESSELLATIONS OF THE ALPHABET

On the dot paper below and on the back of this sheet draw a portion of a tessellation of each of these letters of the alphabet.

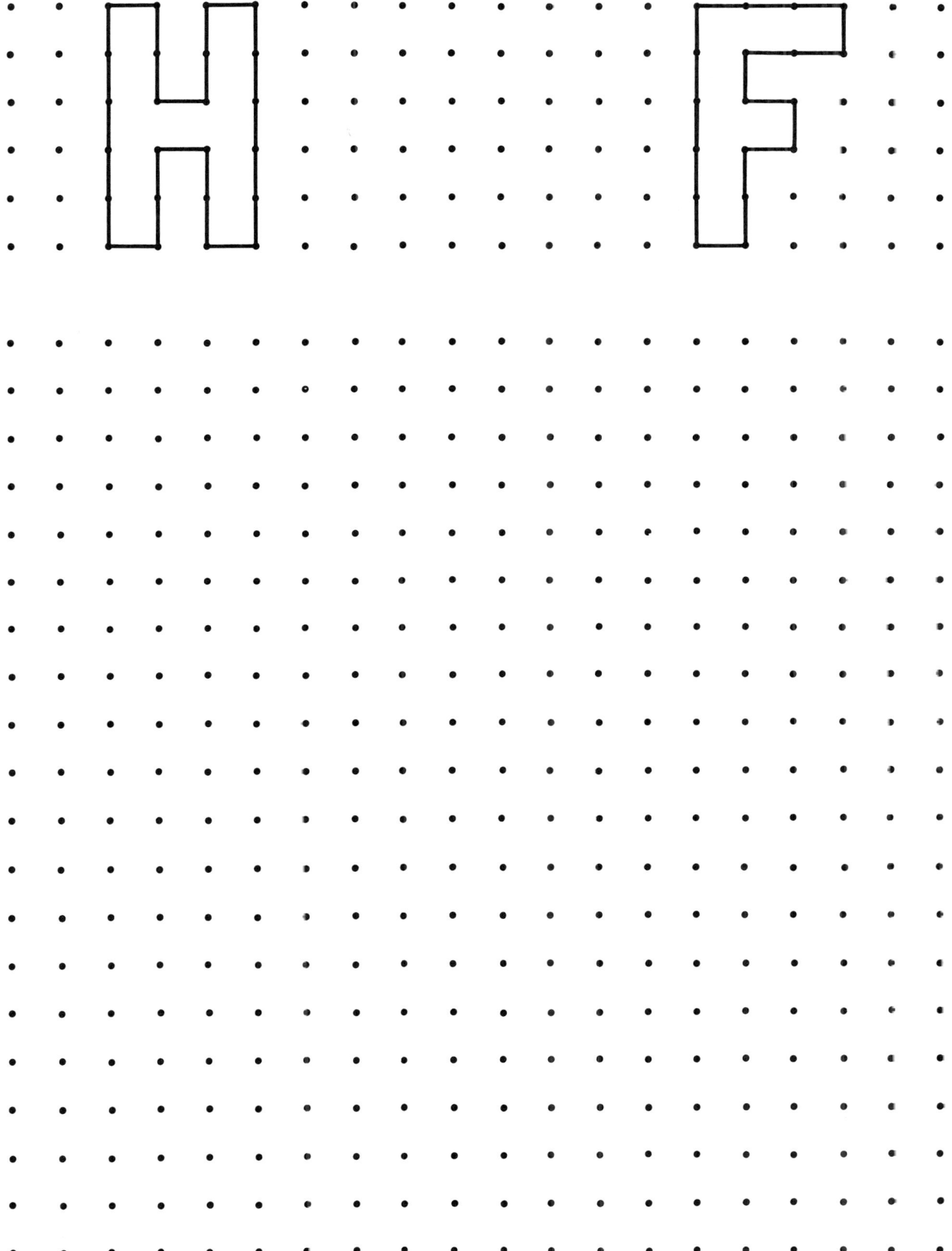

PROBLEM: Find at least two more letters of the alphabet which tessellate.

34 TESSELLATIONS OF THE ALPHABET (continued)

35 TESSELLATIONS OF HEXOMINOES

Show that these hexominoes tessellate by drawing a portion of a tessellation for each. Make sure that you have found a pattern which repeats.

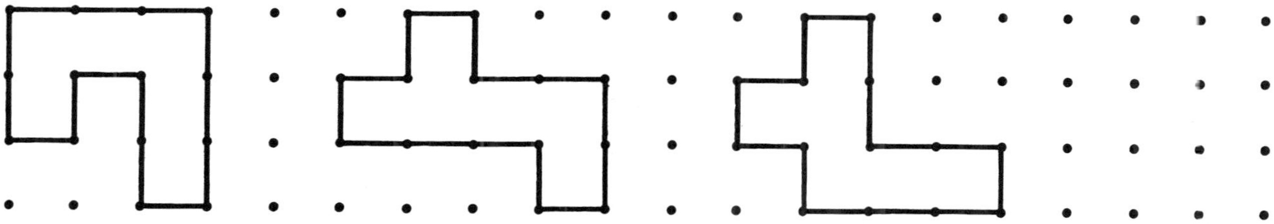

PROBLEM: A hexominoe can be drawn by adding one square to a pentominoe. This can sometimes be done in more than one way. For example, the hexominoe below can be built from exactly two pentominoes.

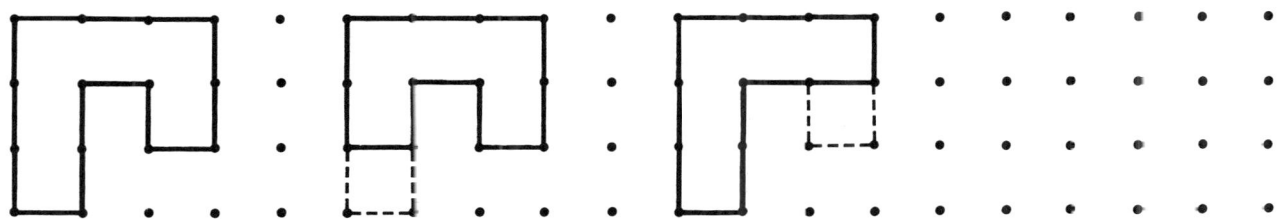

There are at least 14 hexominoes which can be built from exactly three different pentominoes. Draw, on the reverse side, five of these hexominoes and the three pentominoes from which each can be built.

All rights reserved. Addison-Wesley Publishing Company

35 TESSELLATIONS OF HEXOMINOES (continued)

36 TESSELLATIONS WITH COMBINATIONS OF REGULAR POLYGONS

Some combinations of polygons can be arranged to fit exactly around a point with no overlapping. Below we see an example and a nonexample of this.

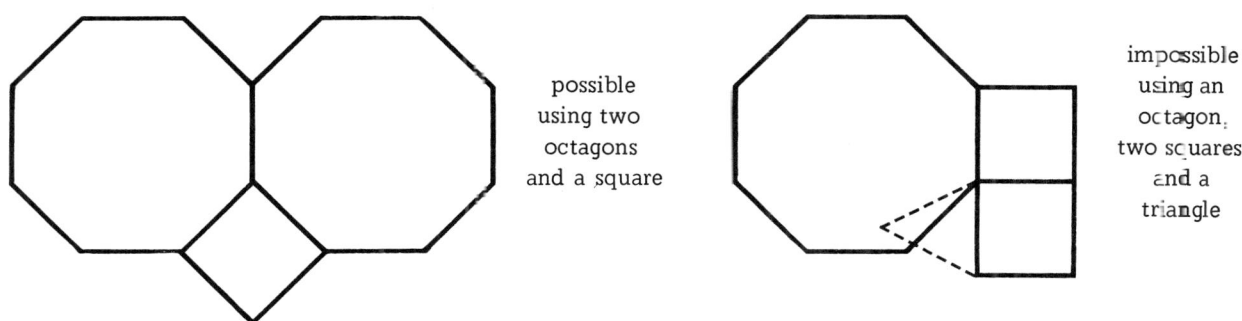

possible using two octagons and a square

impossible using an octagon, two squares, and a triangle

Use the regular polygon shapes below as templates and cut out four copies of each. Using at least two different shapes find all the combinations of these shapes that completely surround a point *P* with no overlapping.

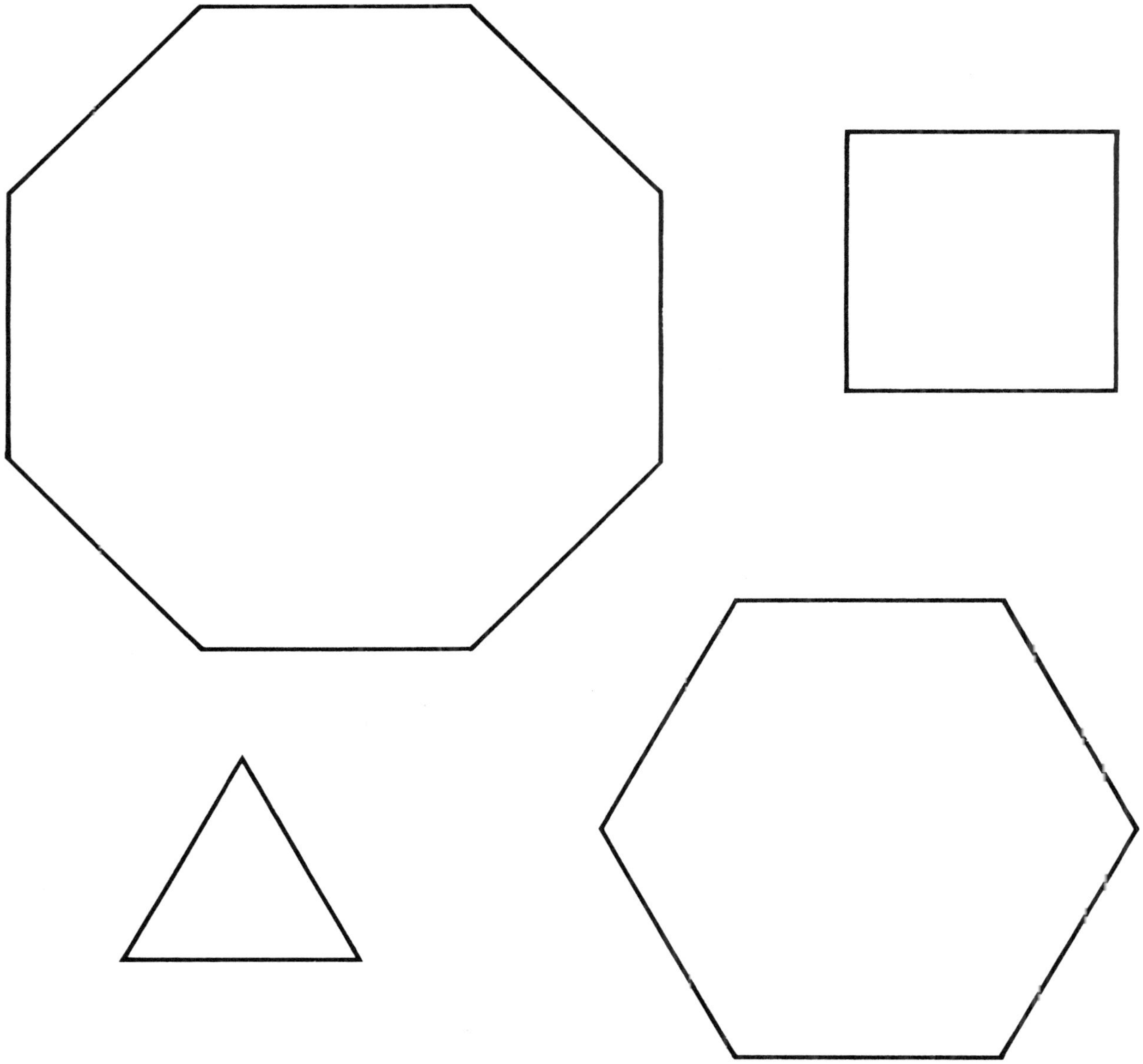

36   TESSELLATIONS WITH COMBINATIONS OF REGULAR POLYGONS (continued)

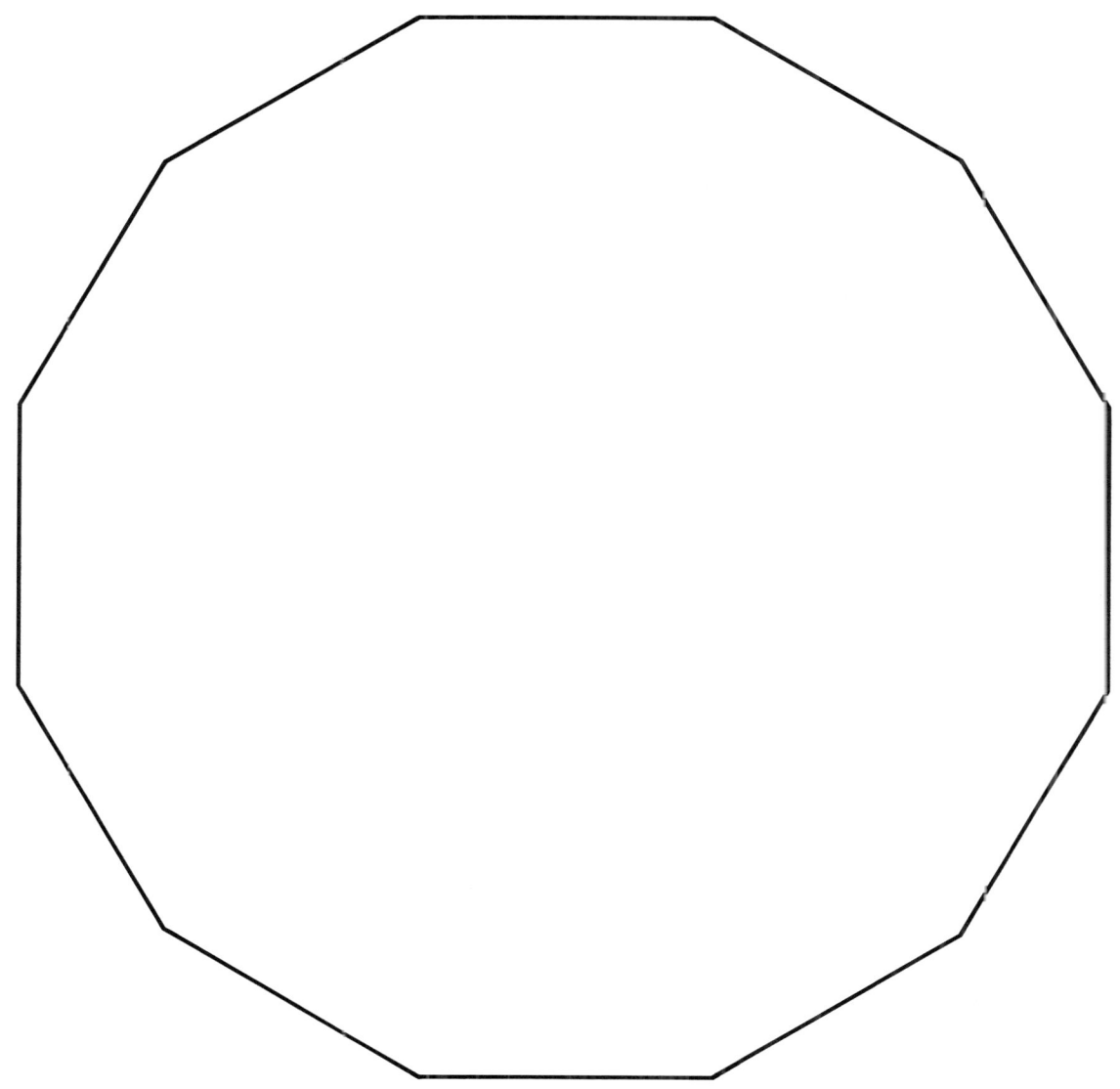

PROBLEM: There exist exactly eight tessellations from two or more different-shaped regular polygons. Which eight of the vertex arrangements found in the first part of this investigation are a part of these eight tessellations?

37 DUAL TESSELLATION OF A REGULAR TESSELLATION

Draw with red pencil a new tessellation from each of these by joining the centers of polygons that share a common side. These new tessellations are called the *dual* of the original tessellations. What new tessellations do you obtain?

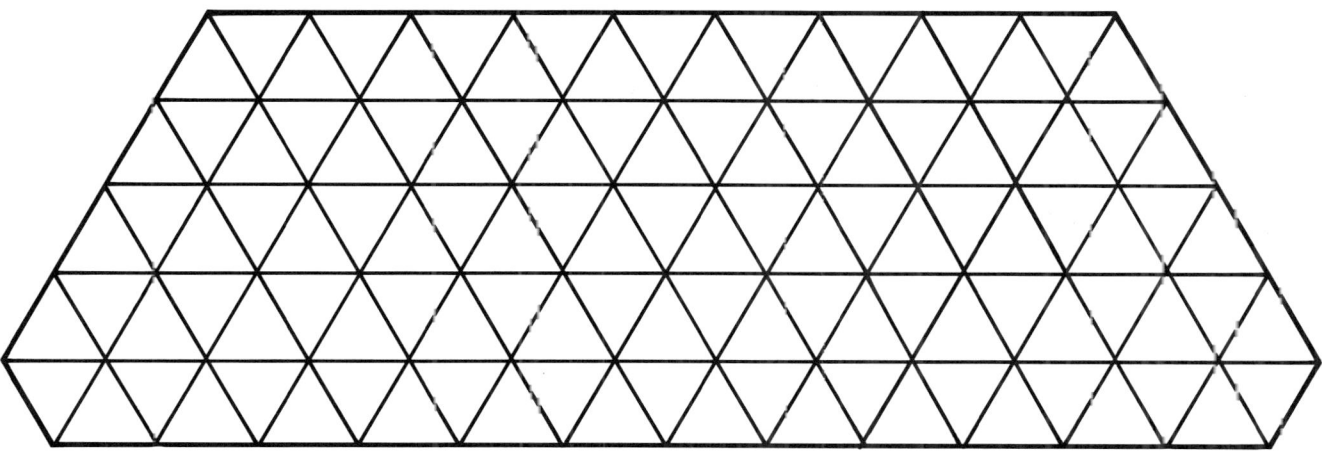

PROBLEM: The dual of the regular tessellation of hexagons is the regular tessellation of equilateral triangles. How does the area of one hexagon compare with the area of one triangle in the dual tessellation?

38 DUAL TESSELLATION OF TRIANGLES

Join the centroids of all triangles with a common edge to form the dual of this tessellation of triangles. (Colored pencils are recommended.)

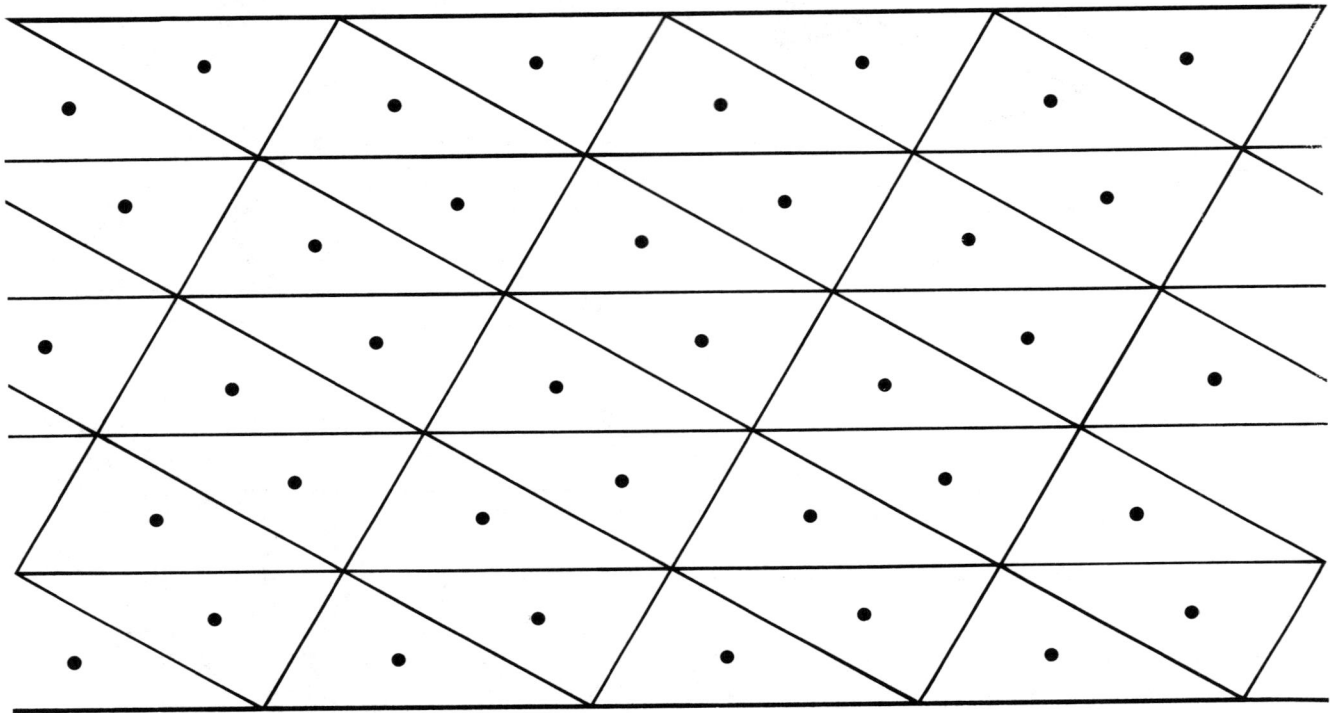

PROBLEM: Conjecture at least one theorem about duals of tessellations of triangles (based on the experience of this investigation) and one theorem about tessellations of hexagons.

39 DUAL TESSELLATION OF A SEMIREGULAR TESSELLATION

Draw the dual of this tessellation with a colored pencil.

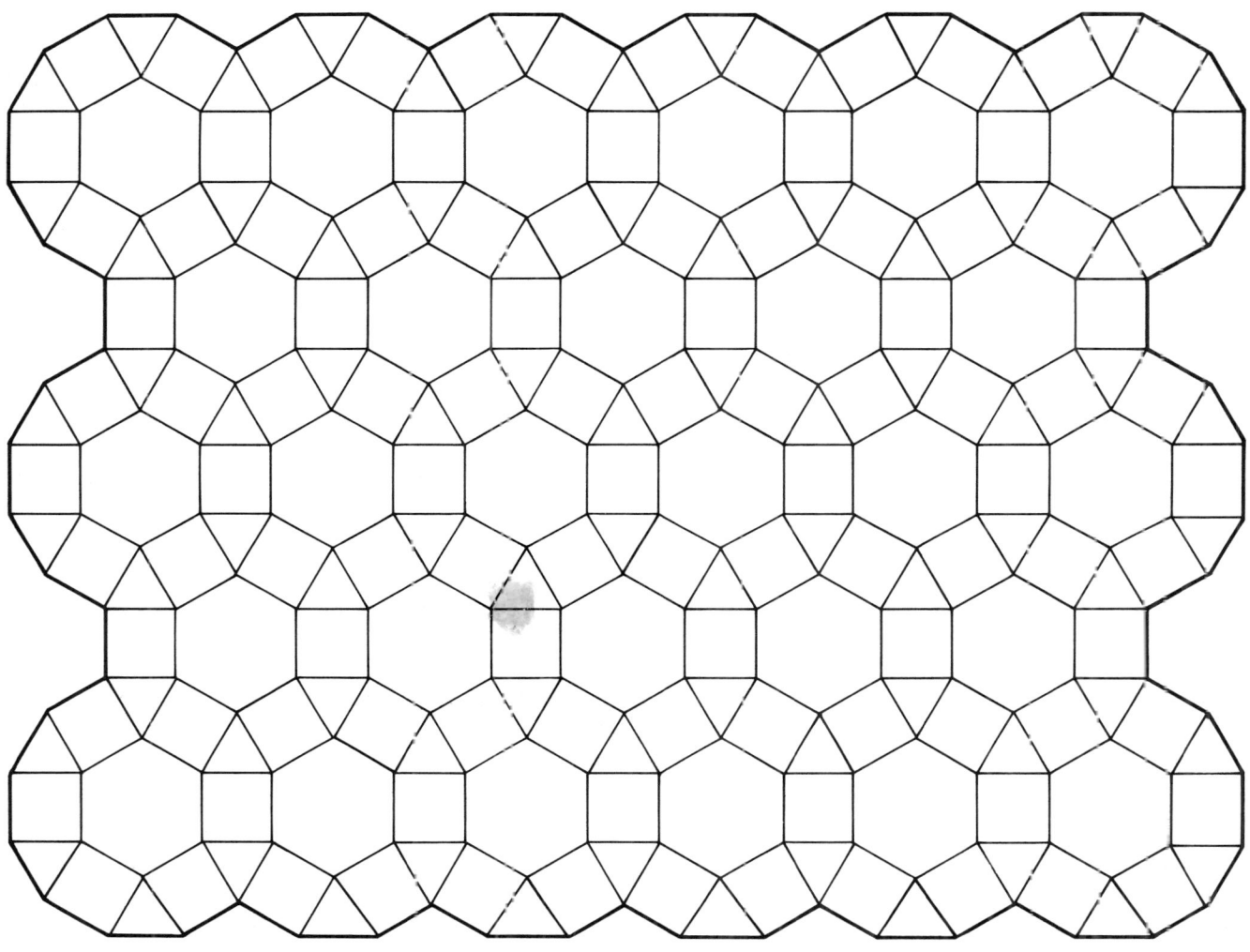

PROBLEM: If the edge of each polygon in the tessellation above is 1, what is the perimeter of each polygon in its dual?

40 DUAL TESSELLATION OF A SEMIREGULAR TESSELLATION

Draw the dual of this tessellation with a colored pencil.

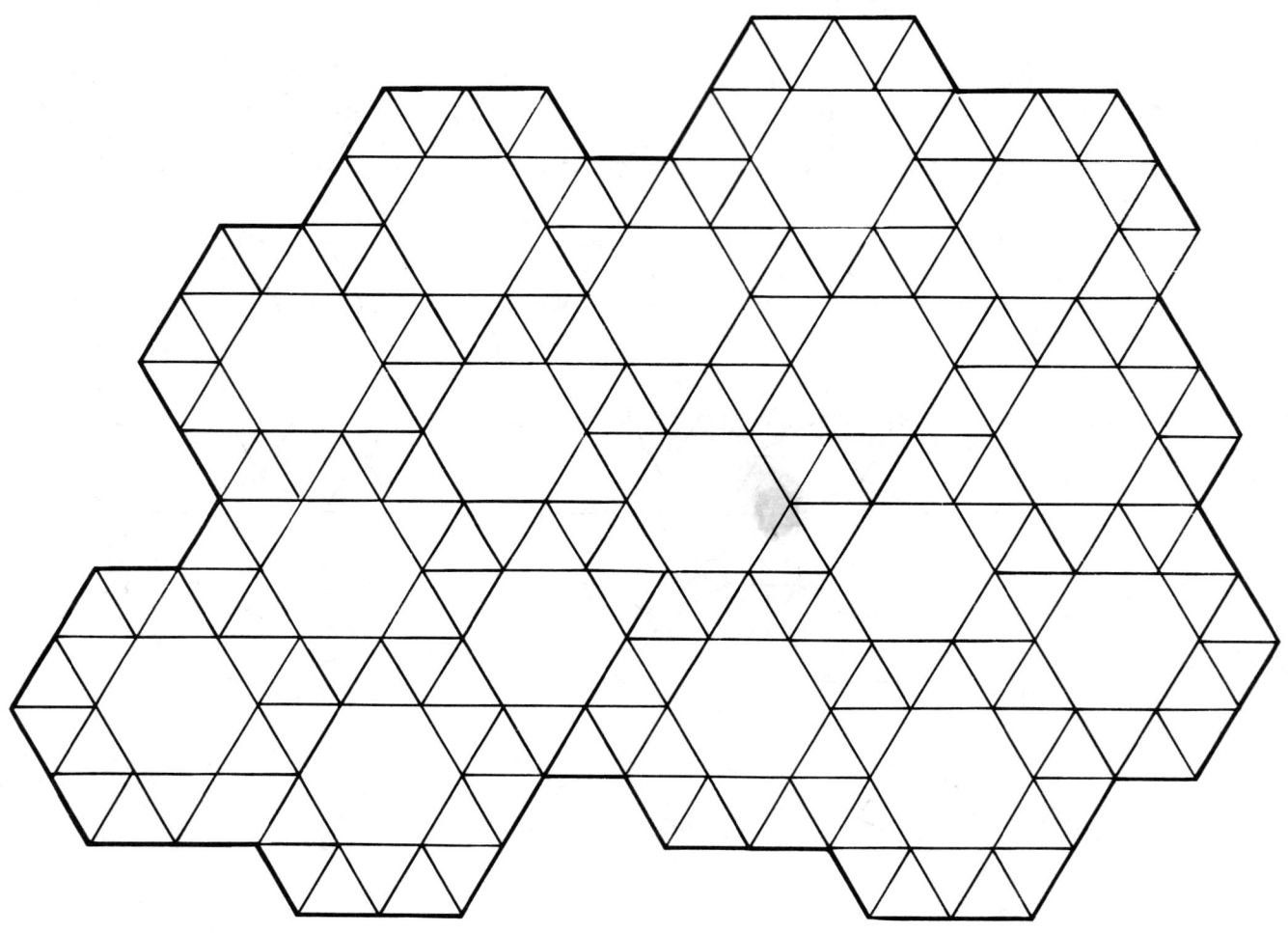

PROBLEM: If the area on one equilateral triangle in this tessellation is 1, what is the area of one pentagon of the dual tessellation?

41 REFLECTIONAL SYMMETRY OF A TESSELLATION

Assume that the tessellation below is extended throughout the entire plane. There are many lines of reflectional symmetry for this tessellation. Use colored pencils and draw all lines of symmetry, making two lines the same color if and only if the lines are parallel. How many colors are required?

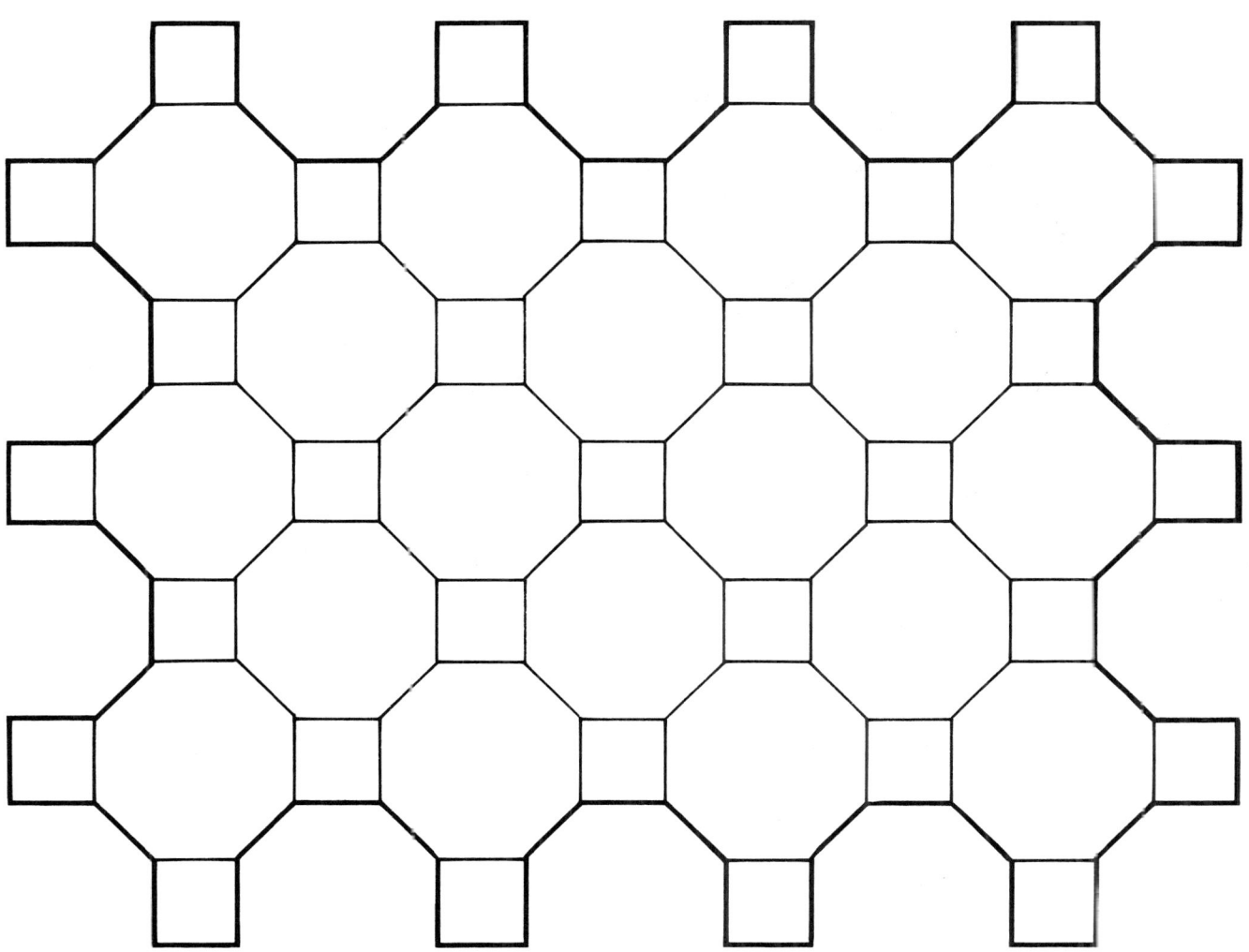

PROBLEM: Assume that the length of the side of a square in the above tessellation is 1. For each color of line find the minimum distance between two symmetry lines of that color.

All rights reserved. Addison-Wesley Publishing Company

42 ROTATIONAL SYMMETRY OF A TESSELLATION

Assume that the tessellation below has been extended throughout the plane. Use colored pencils to draw in all centers of rotational symmetry, making two centers the same color if and only if they are centers of the same order. (A center of rotation has order *n* if 360/*n* is the smallest angle for which the rotation maps the tessellation onto itself.)

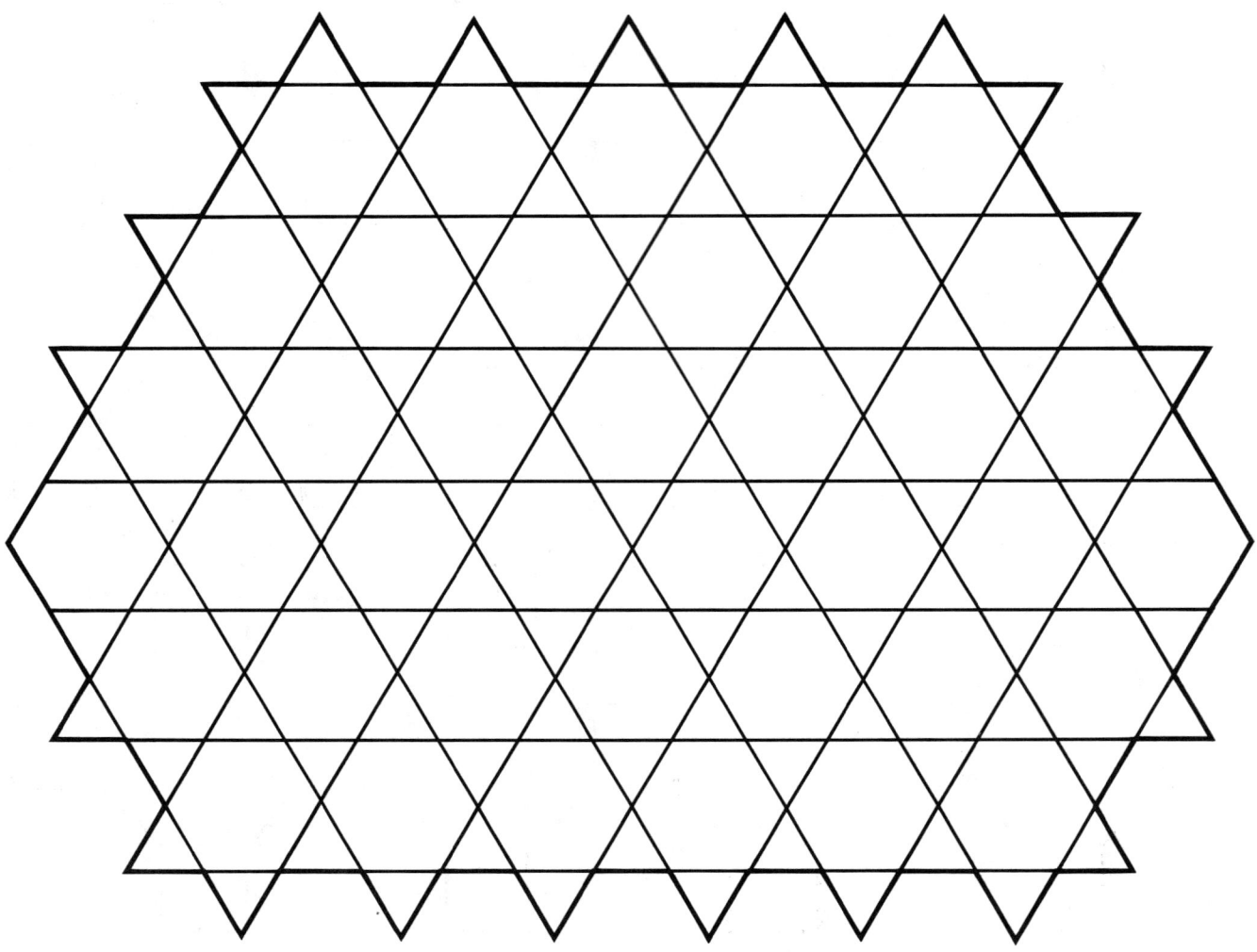

PROBLEM: Assume that the length of the side of the triangle in the above tessellation is 1. What is the minimum distance between centers of symmetry of the first color? Between centers of symmetry of the second color? Between centers of symmetry of the third color?

43 COLORING TESSELLATIONS

Color this tessellation according to some interesting pattern.

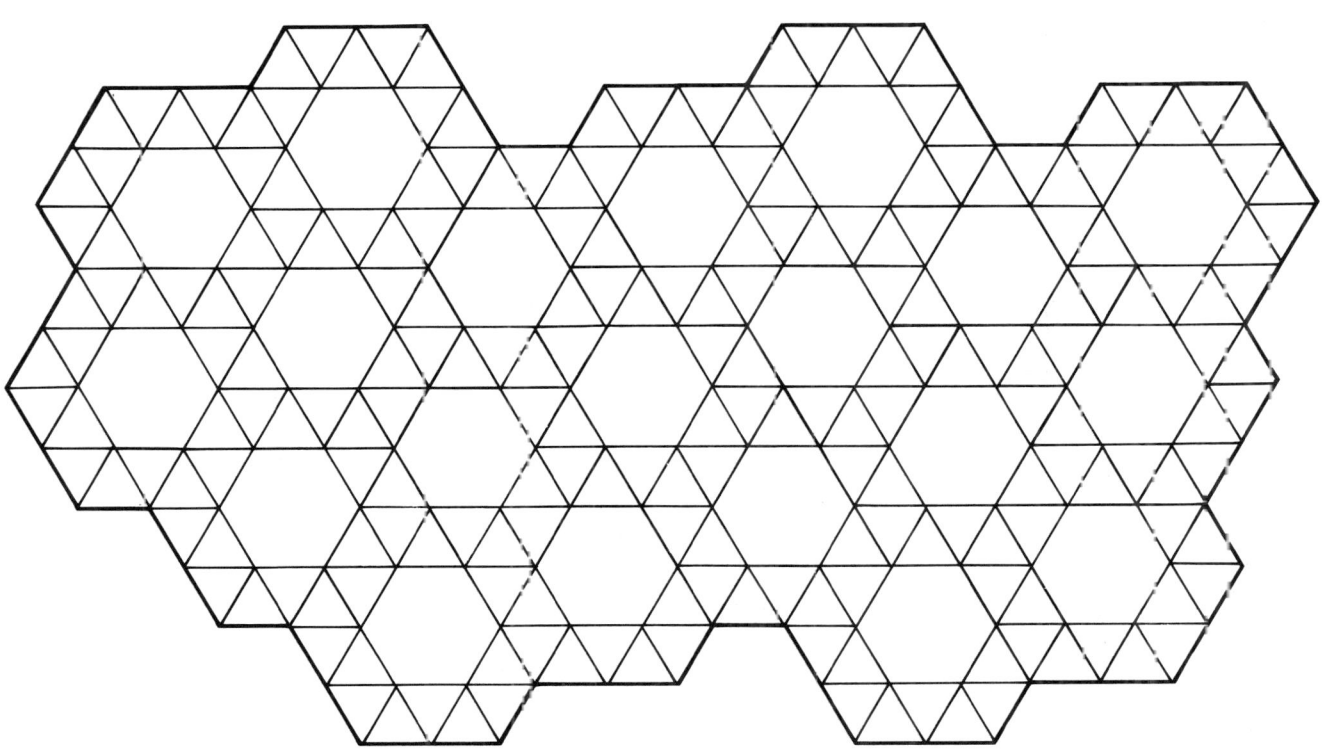

Color this tessellation according to some pattern **different** from the first.

All rights reserved. Addison-Wesley Publishing Company

44 COLORING TESSELLATIONS

Color this tessellation so that polygons with a common *edge* are colored differently. What is the fewest number of colors required for this type of coloring—two, three, four, or five?

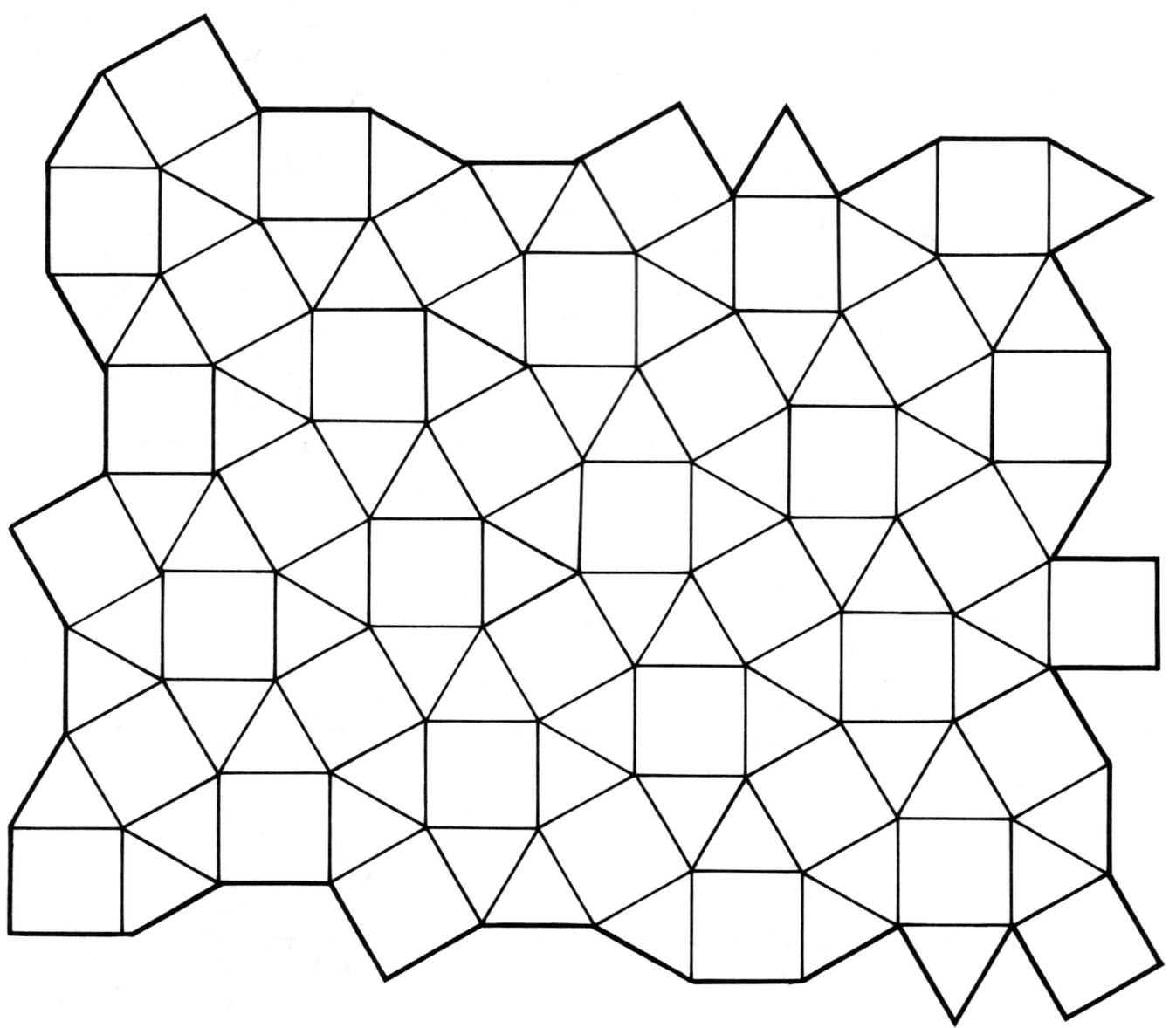

PROBLEM: Does your colored tessellation possess any rotational symmetry?

45 COLORING TESSELLATIONS

Color this tessellation so that polygons which share a *vertex* are colored differently. What is the fewest number of colors required for this type of coloring—four, five, six, or seven?

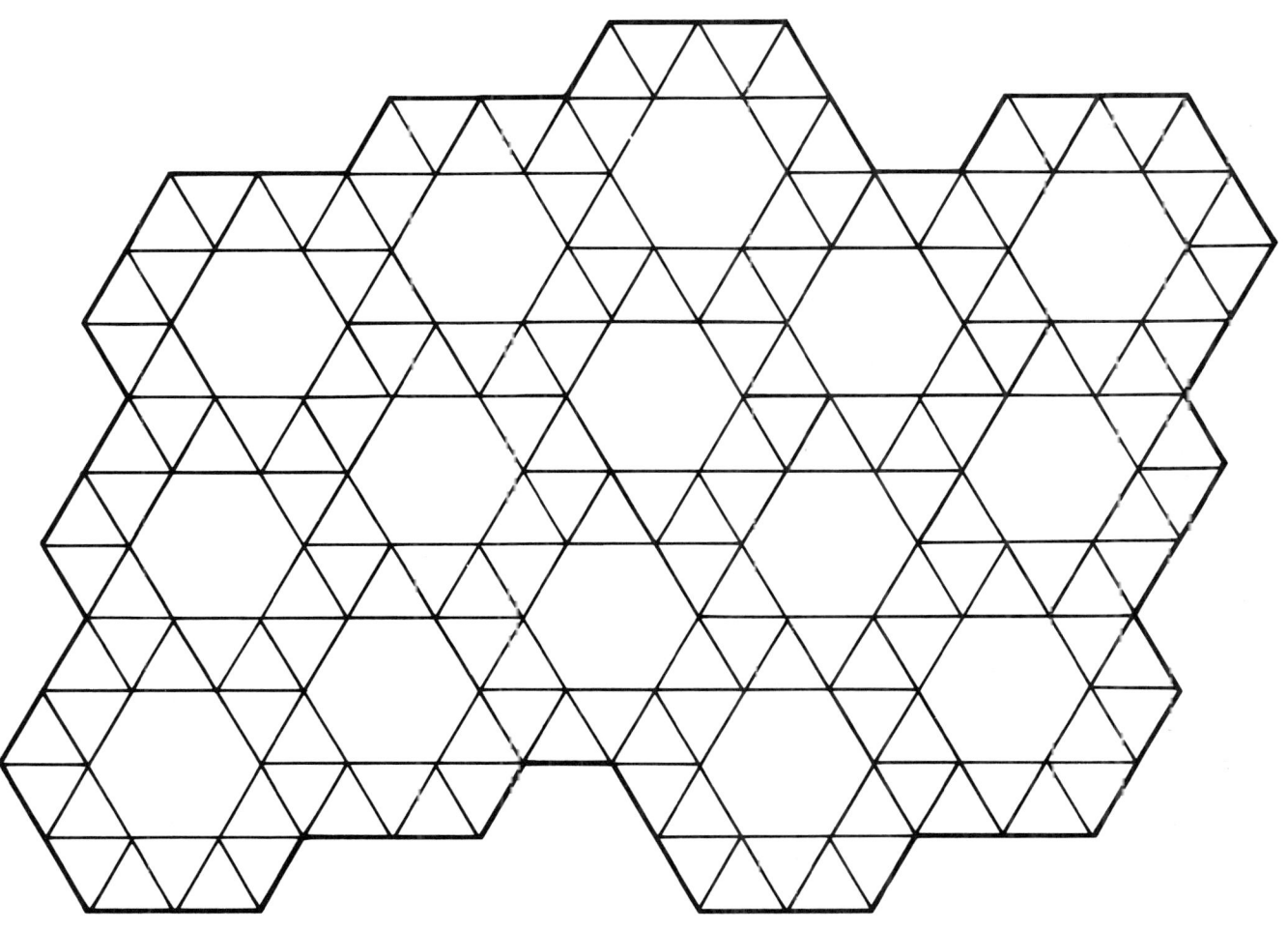

PROBLEM: Does your colored tessellation possess any rotational symmetry?

All rights reserved. Addison-Wesley Publishing Company

46 COLORING TESSELLATIONS

Color the tessellation below so that the lines of reflectional symmetry are emphasized and more easily recognized than in the uncolored tessellation.

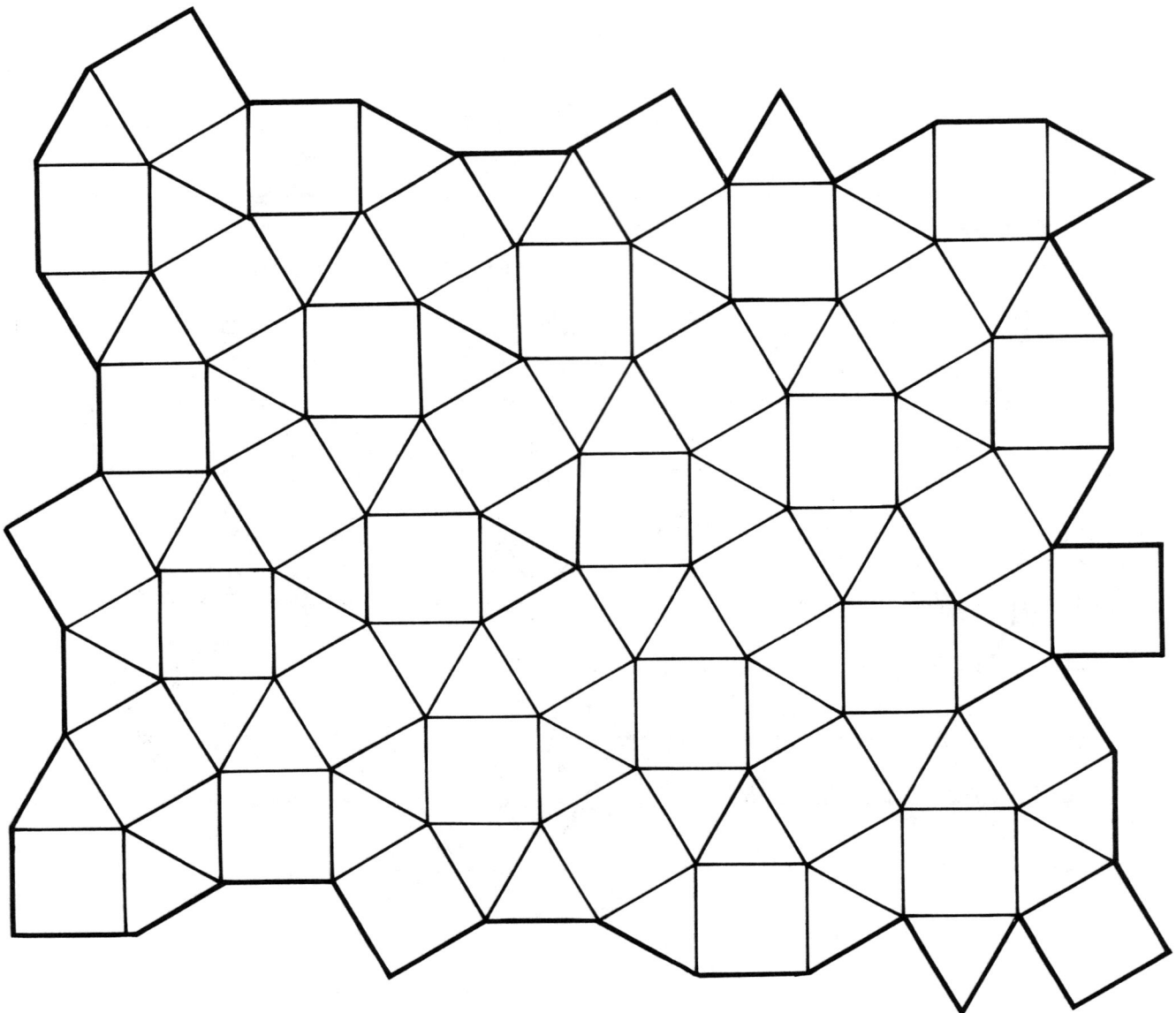

PROBLEM: Does your colored tessellation also possess rotational symmetry?

47 SYMMETRY PROPERTIES OF TESSELLATIONS

Assume that the tessellation below has been extended throughout the entire plane. It possesses many lines of reflectional symmetry and centers of rotational symmetry. If a tessellation is colored and we consider color in identifying lines of reflectional symmetry and centers of rotational symmetry, the colored tessellation may have different symmetry properties from the uncolored tessellation.

Color the tessellation below so that the colored tessellation has fewer lines of symmetry and fewer centers of rotational symmetry than the uncolored tessellation has.

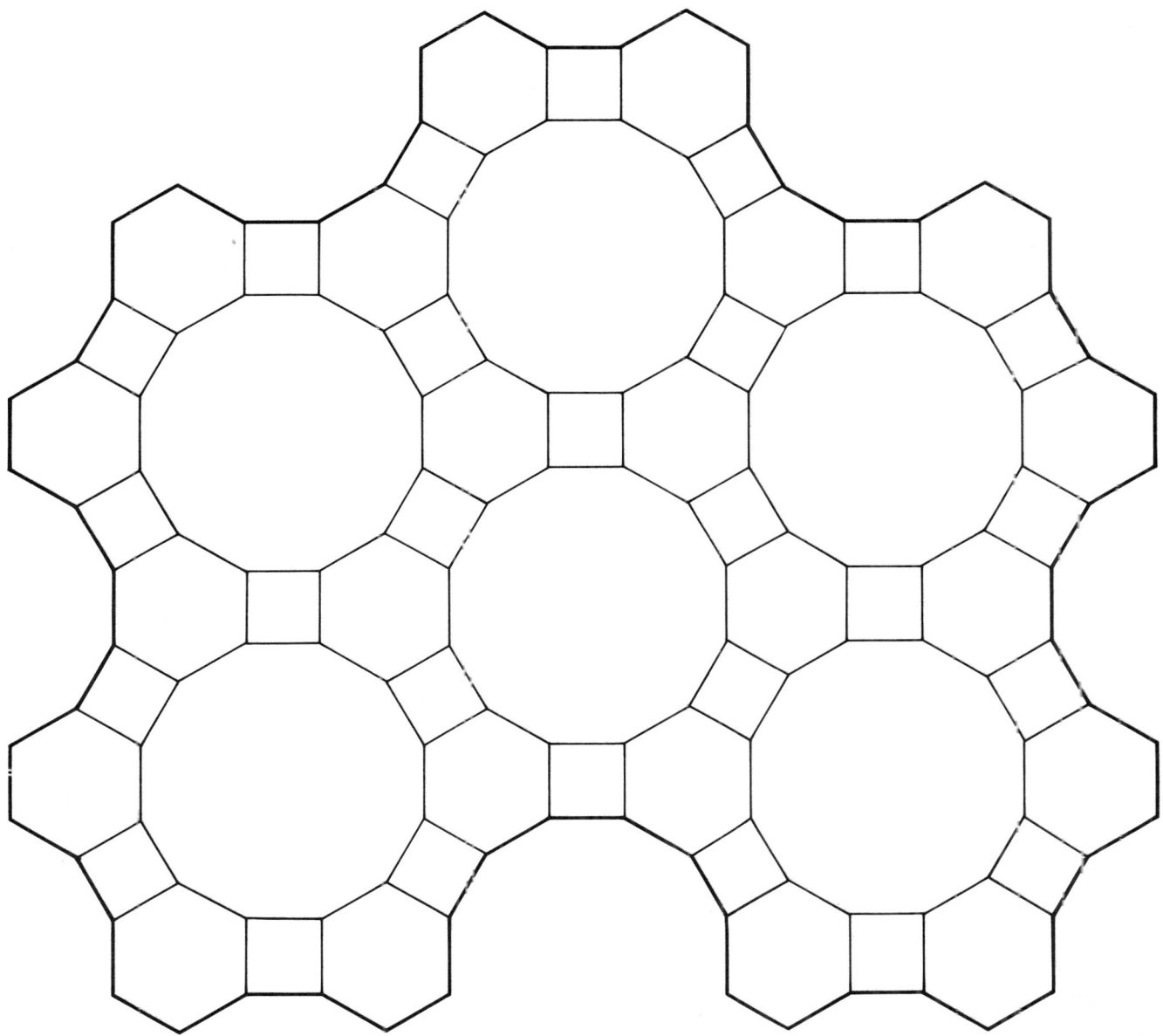

PROBLEM: Can this tessellation be colored so that the colored tessellation has reflectional symmetry but no rotational symmetry? (Use the tessellation on the back of this sheet to answer this question.)

All rights reserved. Addison-Wesley Publishing Company

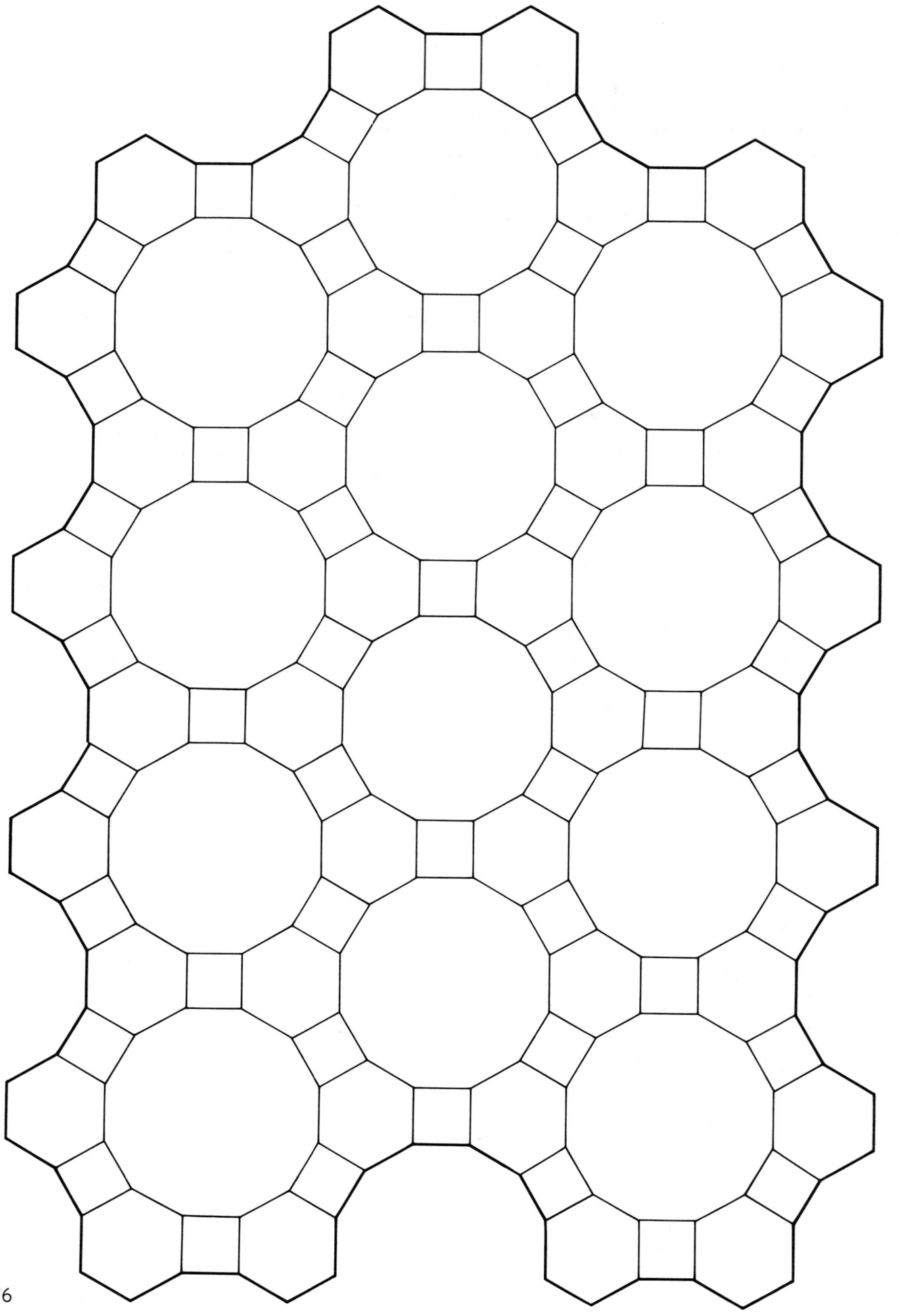

48 TESSELLATIONS OF PENTAGONS

Begin with any triangle and let M be the midpoint of one side. Choose a point P inside the triangle and a point Q so that M is the midpoint of PQ. Then the polygon $ABCPQ$ is a pentagon which tessellates the plane.

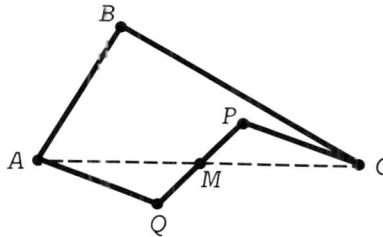

Show that this claim is true by using the method of modifying triangles to pentagons described above for each triangle in the tessellation below. Color the tessellation so that the pentagons are easily recognized.

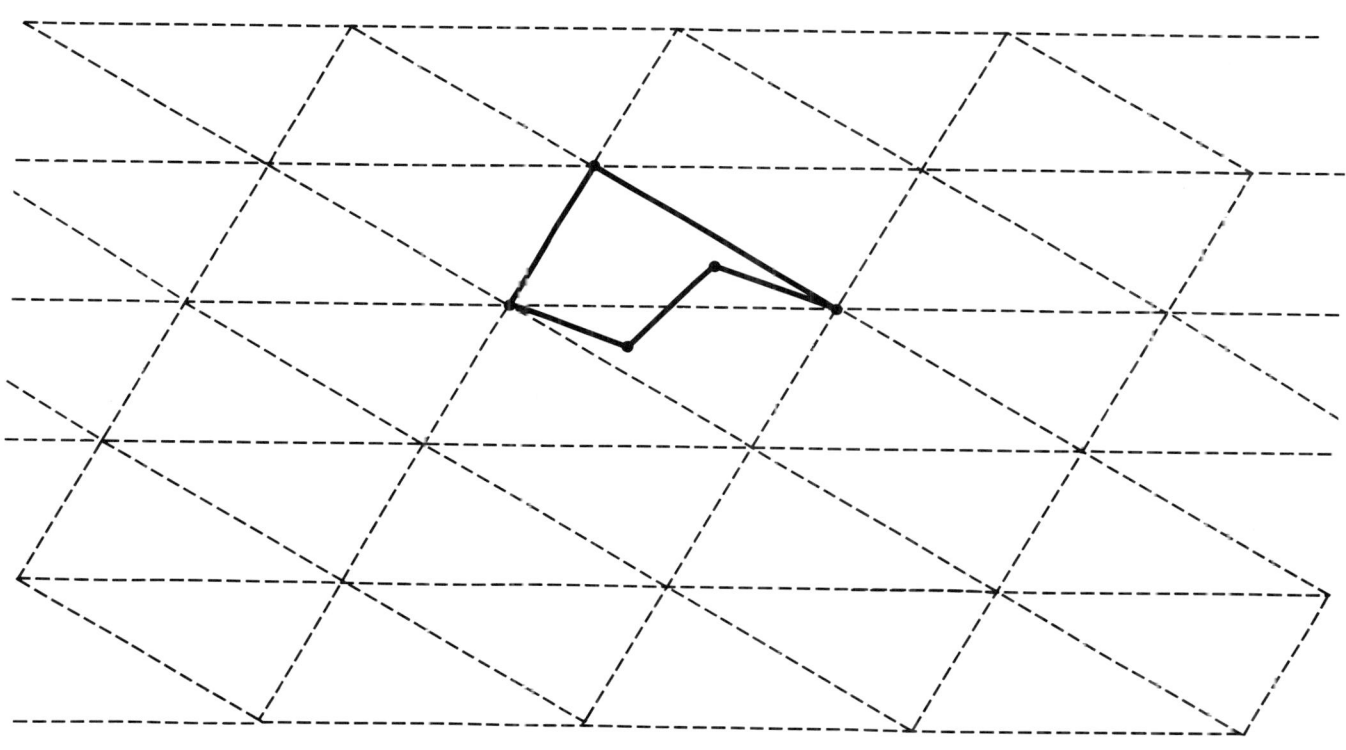

PROBLEM: Find all centers of rotational symmetry for this tessellation of pentagons. Are there any centers of rotational symmetry of the original tessellation of triangles which fail to be centers of rotational symmetry in the tessellation of pentagons?

All rights reserved. Addison-Wesley Publishing Company

49 TESSELLATIONS OF PENTAGONS

The dual tessellation for a few of the semiregular tessellations are tessellations of pentagons. Use a colored pencil to draw the dual of the tessellation below and obtain a tessellation of pentagons.

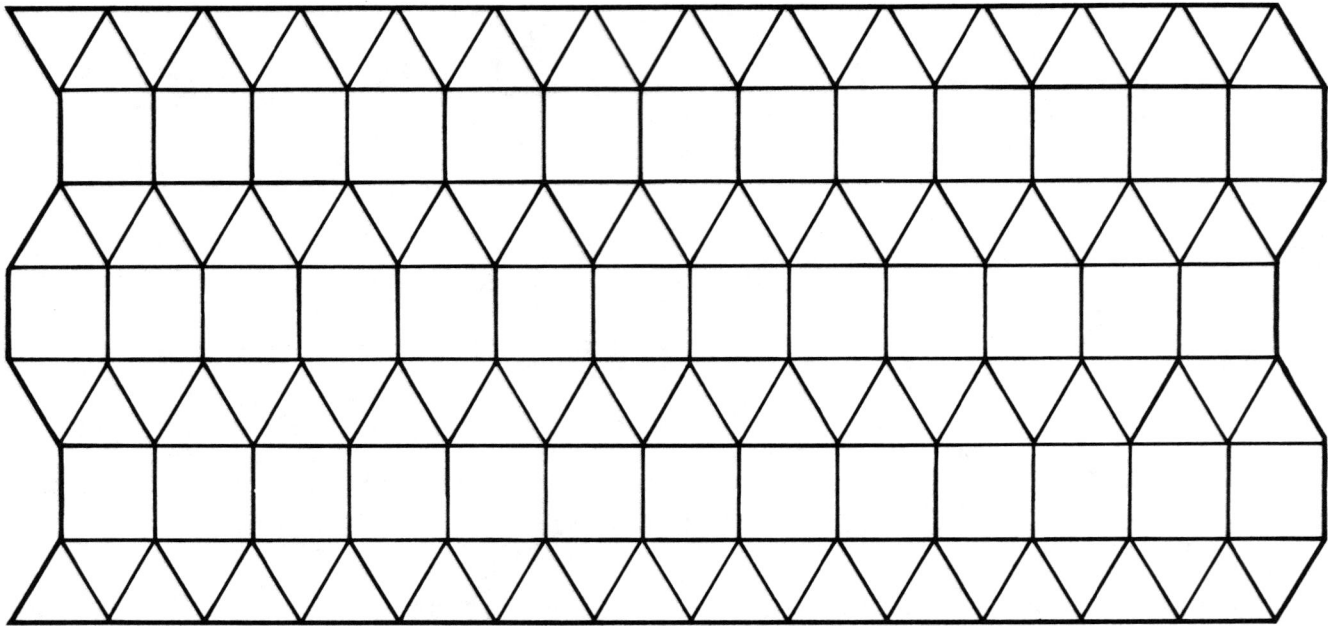

PROBLEM: If the area of one square in the tessellation above is 1, what is the area of one pentagon in the dual tessellation?

50 MORE TESSELLATIONS OF PENTAGONS

Begin with a tessellation of squares and place an "X" in each square so that the "X" of neighboring squares touch, as indicated in the example.

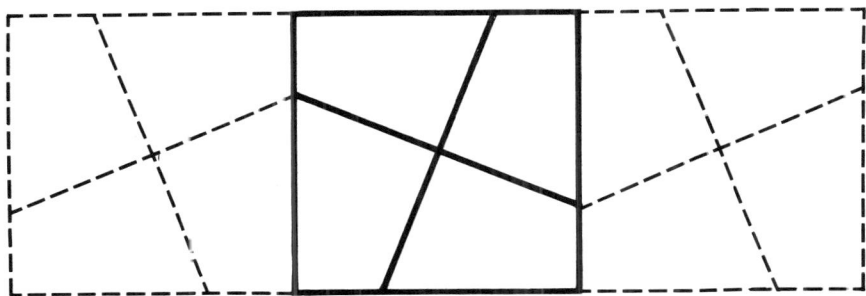

Do this in each square of the following tessellation and show by coloring it how neighboring regions can be joined to yield a tessellation of irregular pentagons which possess exactly one line of symmetry.

PROBLEM: If the area of the squares is one, what is the area of the pentagons you obtained? (Hint: No calculation is required.)

51 TESSELLATIONS OF HEXAGONS

You can put two congruent quadrilaterals together to form a hexagon as shown in this example.

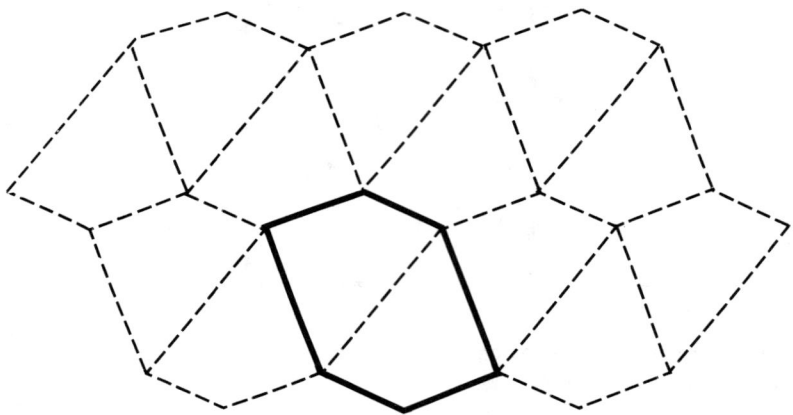

In each portion of the tessellation below draw a different shaped hexagon by tracing around adjoining quadrilaterals with a colored pencil. Draw enough of the hexagons to show that they tessellate the plane.

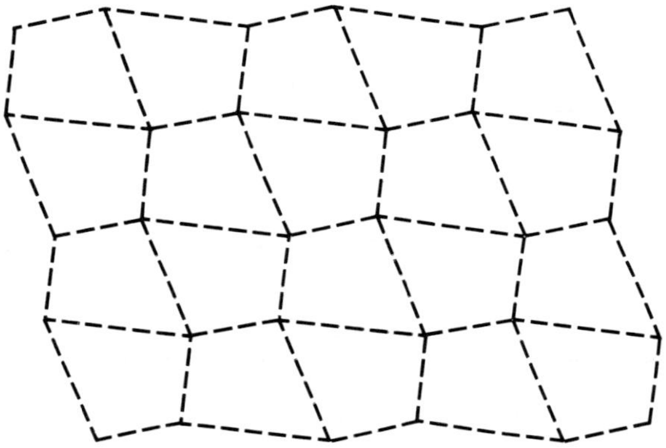

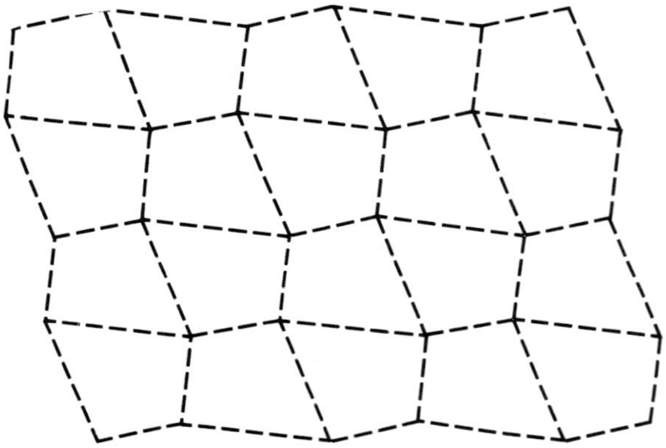

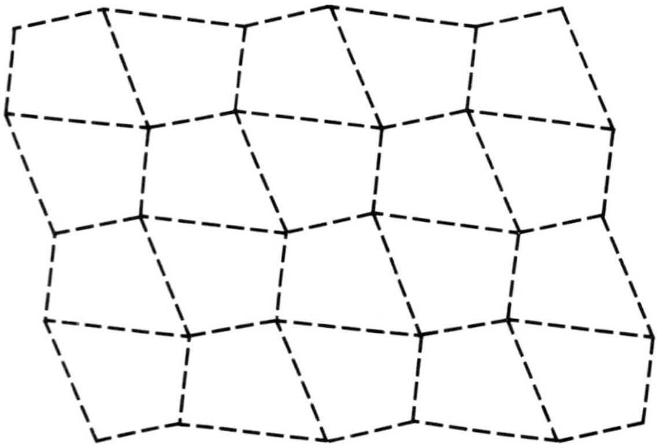

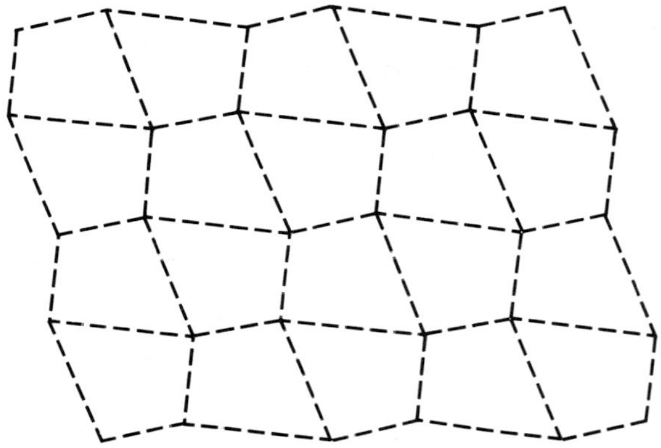

PROBLEM: Given a hexagon with all pairs of opposite sides parallel, how many of its diagonals divide the hexagon into a pair of congruent quadrilaterals?

(Notice that this says that all hexagons with opposite sides parallel can be obtained from several tessellations of quadrilaterals by using the method of this investigation. We conclude that all hexagons of this type tessellate the plane.)

52 TESSELLATIONS OF HEXAGONS

Begin with any parallelogram *KLMN* and select points *X* and *Y* in the interior of the parallelogram. Let *A* and *B* be the points so that *K* is the midpoint of *AX* and *L* is the midpoint of *BX*, and let *C* and *D* be the points so that *M* is the midpoint of *CY* and *N* is the midpoint of *DY*. Then *AXBCYD* is a hexagon which tessellates the plane.

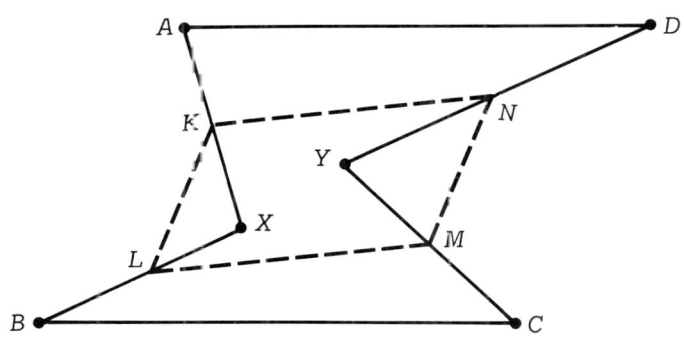

Demonstrate that these hexagons tessellate by repeating the above construction for each of the points *X* and *Y* in the tessellation below.

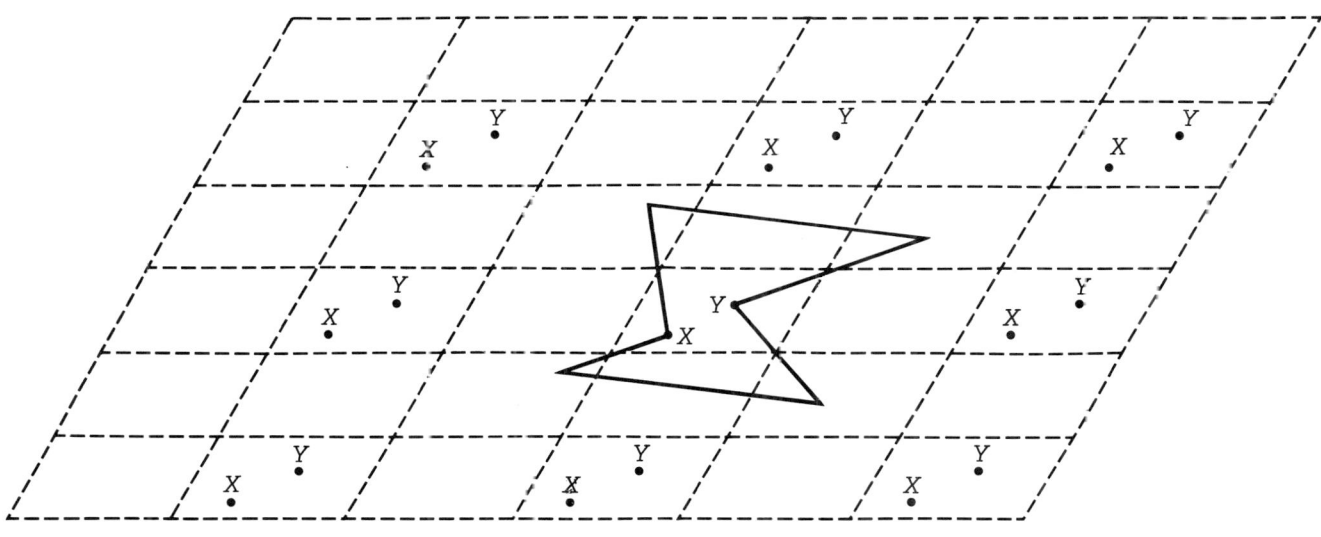

PROBLEM: Show that the area of one hexagon in the above tessellation is twice the area of one parallelogram. (No measurement or calculation is required.)

All rights reserved. Addison-Wesley Publishing Company

53 MORE TESSELLATIONS OF HEXAGONS

Begin with any quadrilateral ABCD and let M be the midpoint of CD. Choose a point P inside the quadrilateral and a point Q such that M is the midpoint of PQ. Then the polygon ABCDPQ is a hexagon which tessellates the plane.

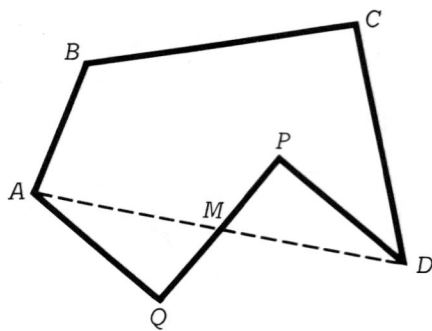

In the tessellation below show that this claim is true by using the method of modifying quadrilaterals to hexagons described above for each quadrilateral. Color the tessellation so that the hexagons are easily recognized.

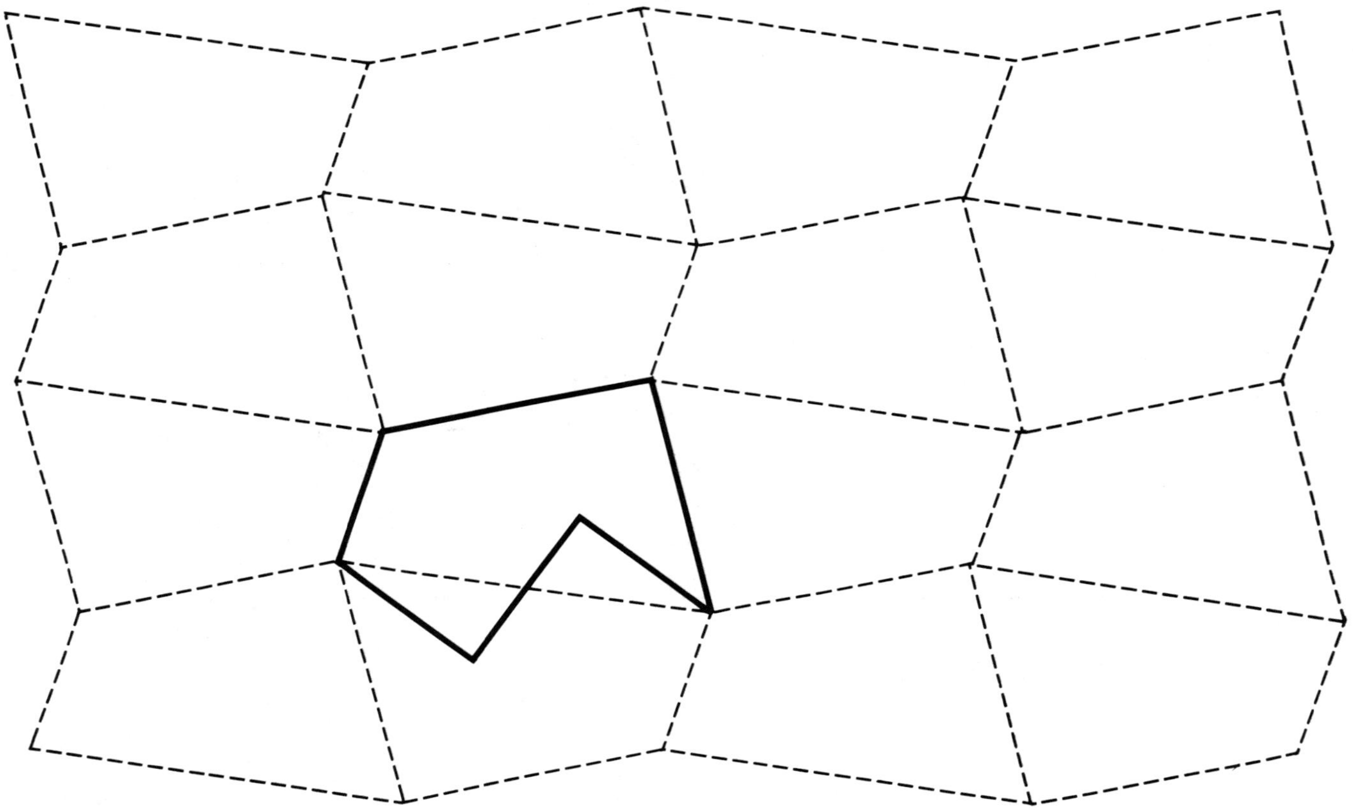

PROBLEM: Find all centers of rotational symmetry for this tessellation of hexagons. Are there any centers of rotational symmetry of the original tessellation of quadrilaterals that fail to be centers of rotational symmetry in the tessellation of hexagons?

54   TESSELLATIONS OF CURVED FIGURES

The pattern in the square given here gives the square 90° rotational symmetry but no reflectional symmetry.

Draw this pattern in each square of the tessellation below.
Color the resulting pattern so that a tessellation of curved figures stands out.

PROBLEM: Select some region in your tessellation bounded by the lines of the tessellation and find the area of the region. (Assume that the area of the square is 1.)

55 TESSELLATIONS OF CURVED FIGURES

One method for making an interesting tessellation of curved figures involves beginning with a tessellation of some polygon and replacing each edge of the polygons with a figure which has 180° symmetry about the midpoint of the edge.

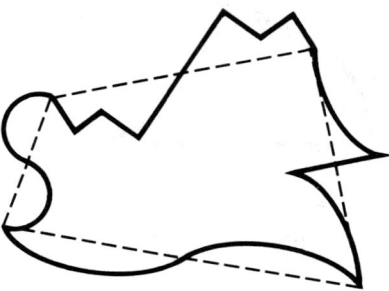

Create a tessellation of curved figures beginning with the tessellation of quadrilaterals below and replace each edge with the curve indicated in the pattern given here.

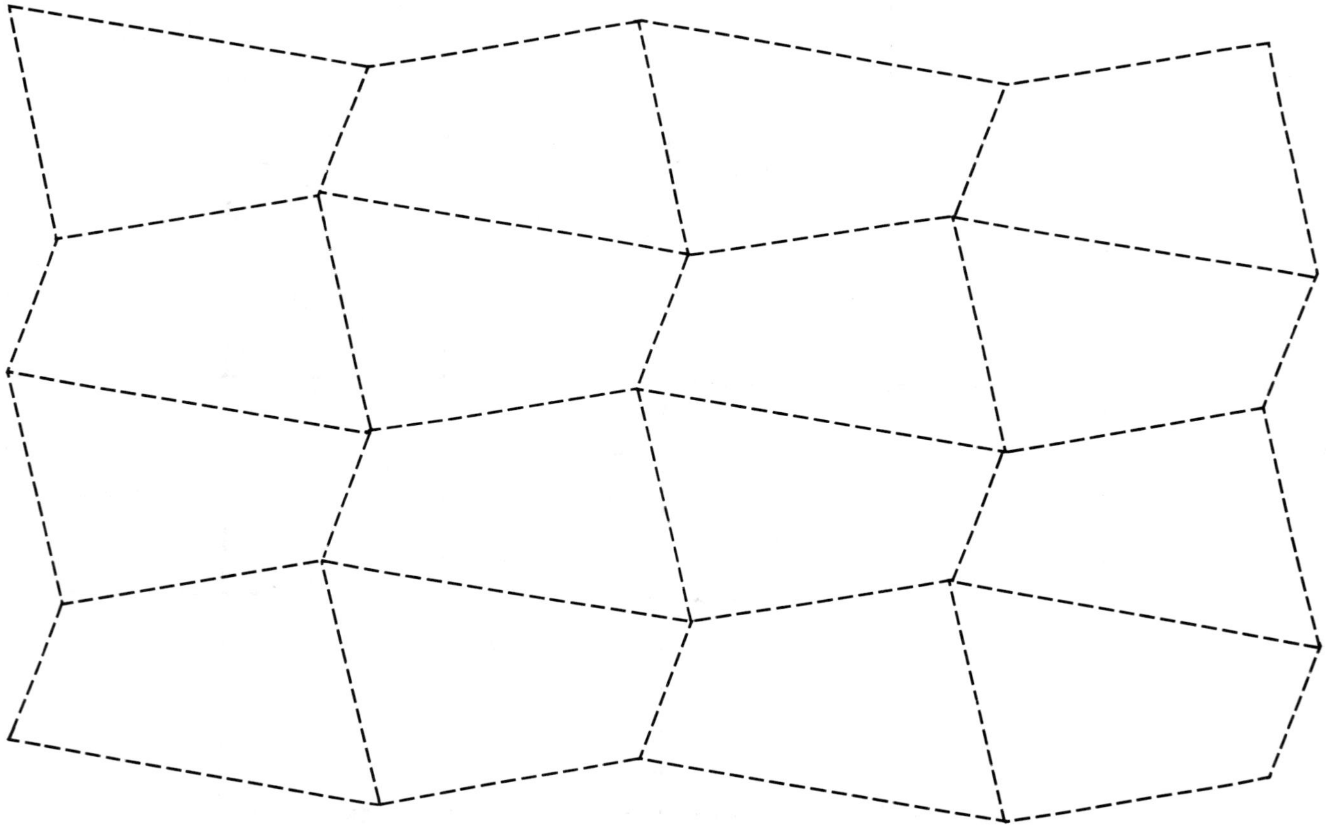

PROBLEM: Repeat the above process using a pattern of your own design. Can you design this pattern to form a tessellation of figures from nature (e.g., birds, fish, or flowers)?

56 TESSELLATIONS AND THE CONSTRUCTION OF DISSECTION PUZZLES

You can use superimposed tessellations as a way of generating puzzles like those of Investigation 7.

Using colored pencil, join the heavy dots in the tessellation below to form a tessellation of parallelograms of the shape given below.

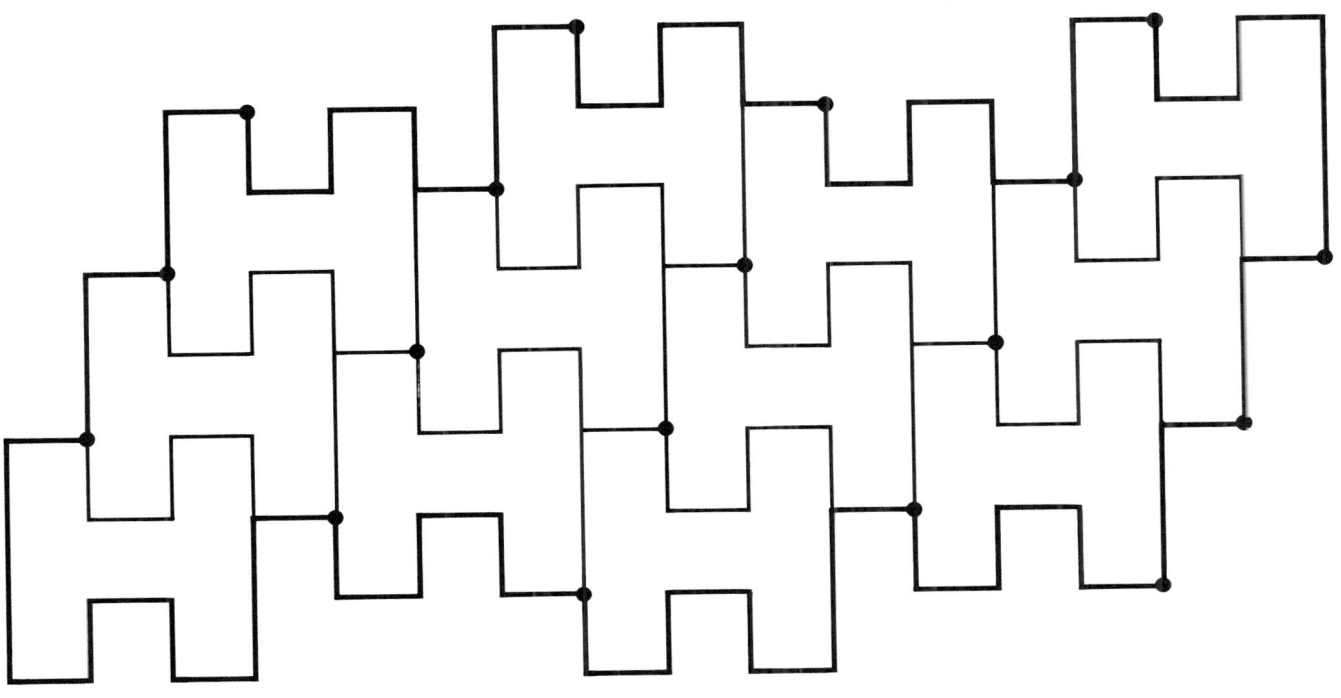

Examine the resulting pattern above to discover why the pieces below fit together to form both the parallelogram and the letter H.

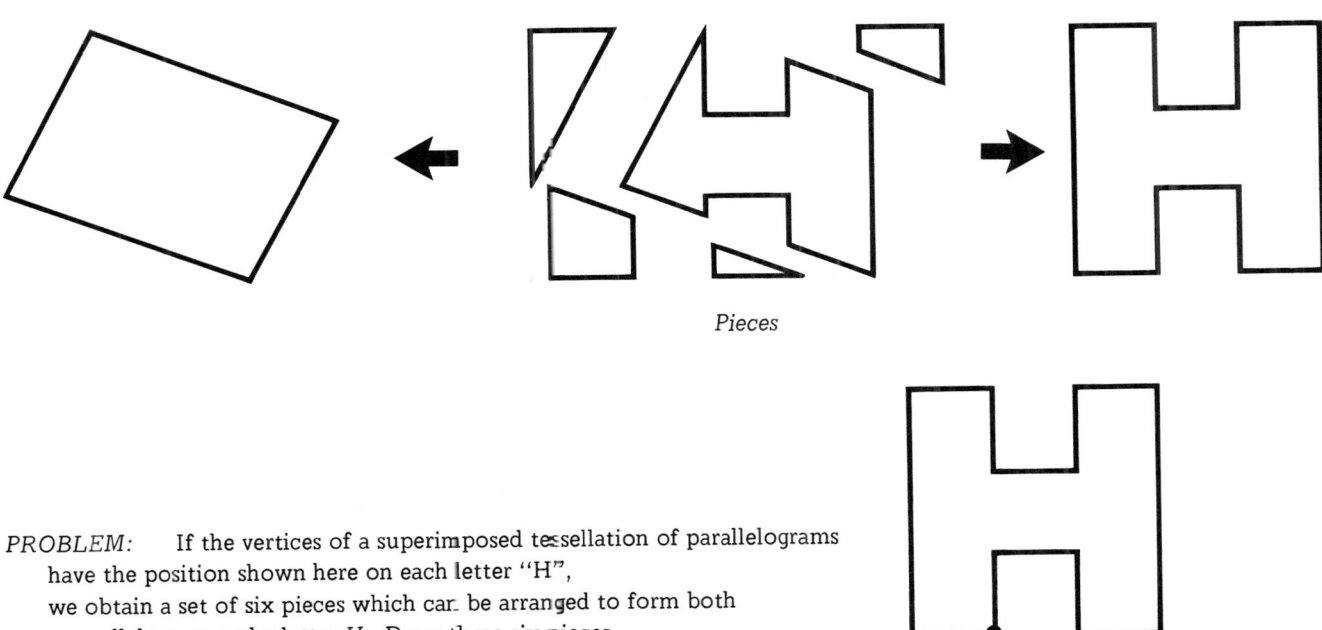

Pieces

PROBLEM: If the vertices of a superimposed tessellation of parallelograms have the position shown here on each letter "H", we obtain a set of six pieces which can be arranged to form both a parallelogram and a letter H. Draw these six pieces.

All rights reserved. Addison-Wesley Publishing Company

57 VERTEX FIGURE TESSELLATION

A vertex figure in a tessellation is a polygon whose vertices are the midpoints of the edges of the basic polygon figures which emanate from a vertex of the tessellation. For example, a vertex figure in the tessellation of regular hexagons is an equilateral triangle.

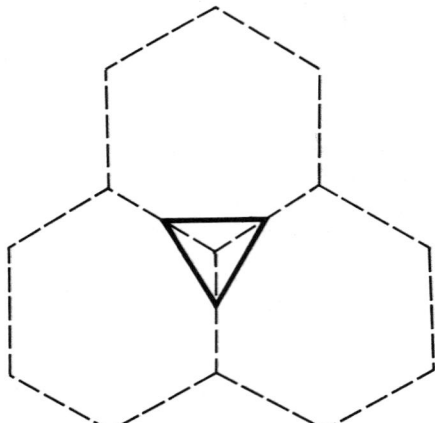

Use a colored pencil to draw all the vertex figures of the tessellation below to obtain a tessellation of triangles, squares, and pentagons.

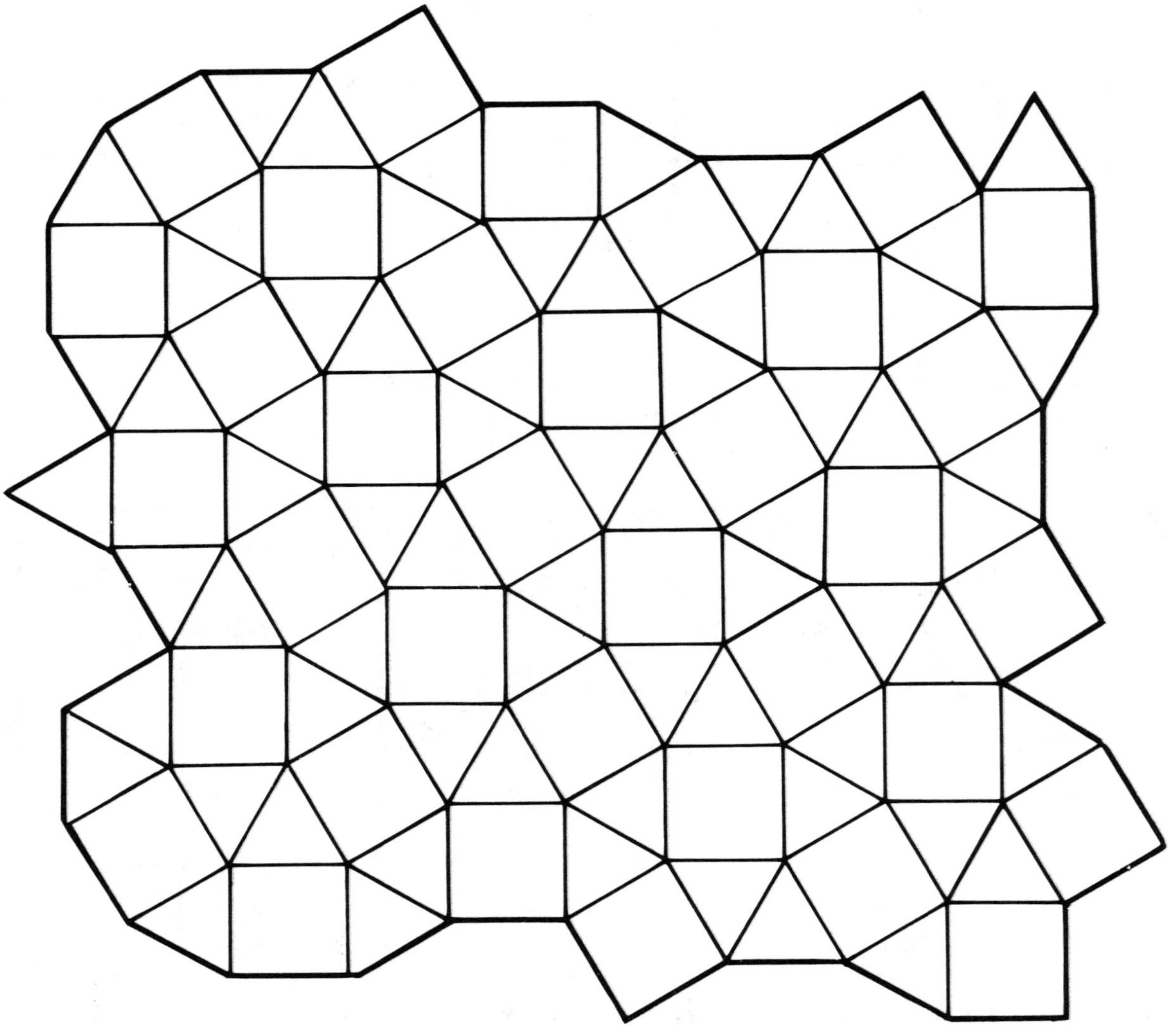

PROBLEM: If the area of a square in the original tessellation is 1, what is the area of the triangle, square, and pentagon in the vertex figure tessellation?

58 THREE-MIRROR KALEIDOSCOPE TESSELLATIONS

Draw in one color those lines of symmetry of this tessellation that do not pass through the triangles. Draw in a second color those lines of symmetry that pass through the triangles.

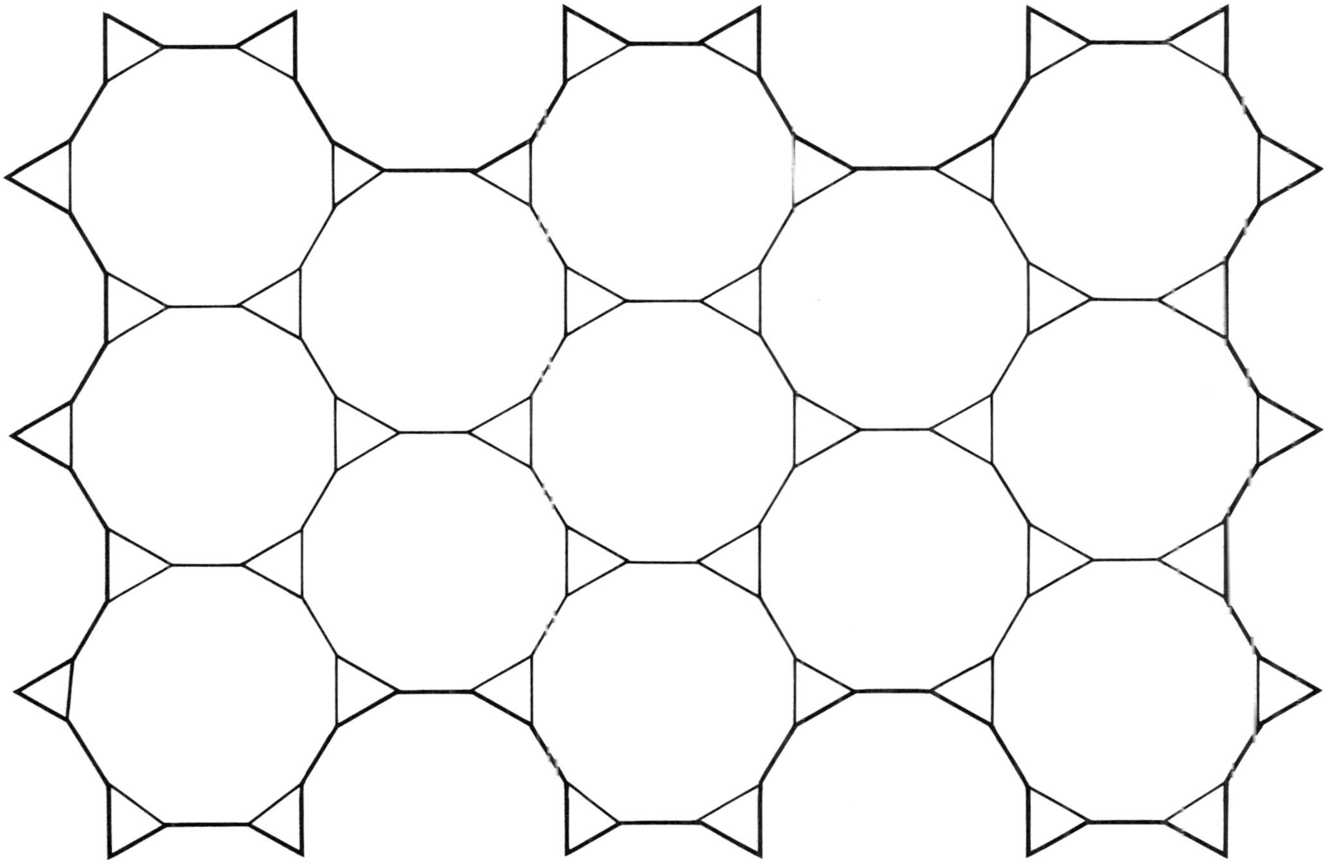

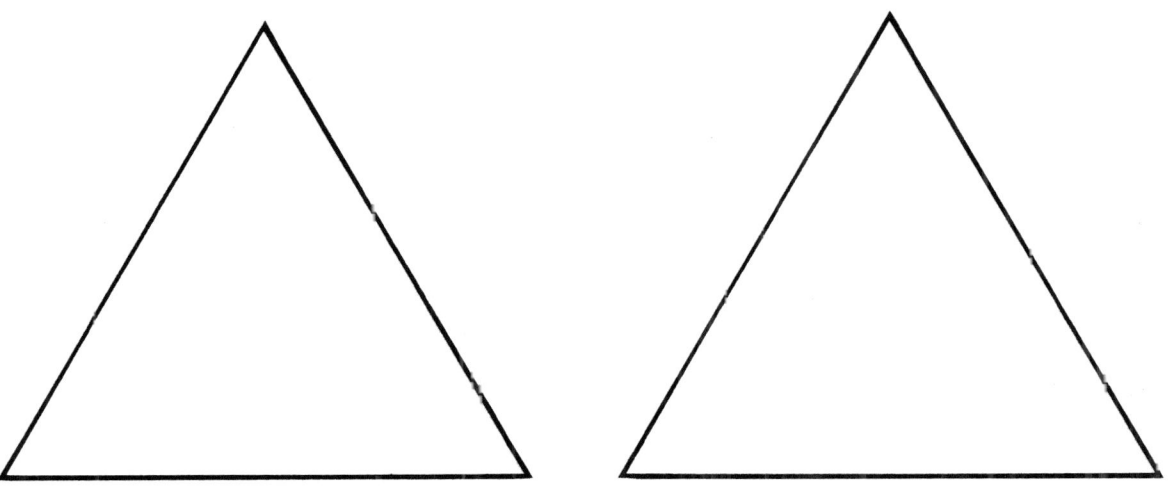

Patterns which correspond to the triangular regions formed by the lines of symmetry of one color can be placed in the base of a three-mirror kaleidoscope in order to generate the tessellation above. Sketch these two patterns in the triangles below.

PROBLEM: Suppose construction paper is used to make patterns for the base of a three-mirror kaleidoscope. Which one of the two patterns above will always generate a tessellation with all triangles the same color, and which one could be used to generate a tessellation with triangles of two colors?

59 CREATING TESSELLATIONS

Draw on this dot paper an interesting tessellation.

PROBLEM: Does your tessellation possess any symmetry?
If so, change its symmetry properties by coloring.

60 CONSTRUCTING REGULAR POLYHEDRA

Use the patterns below as templates for posterboard cutouts. Make a polyhedron (attaching cutouts with rubber bands) using 20 triangular faces, one with six square faces, and one with 12 pentagon faces.

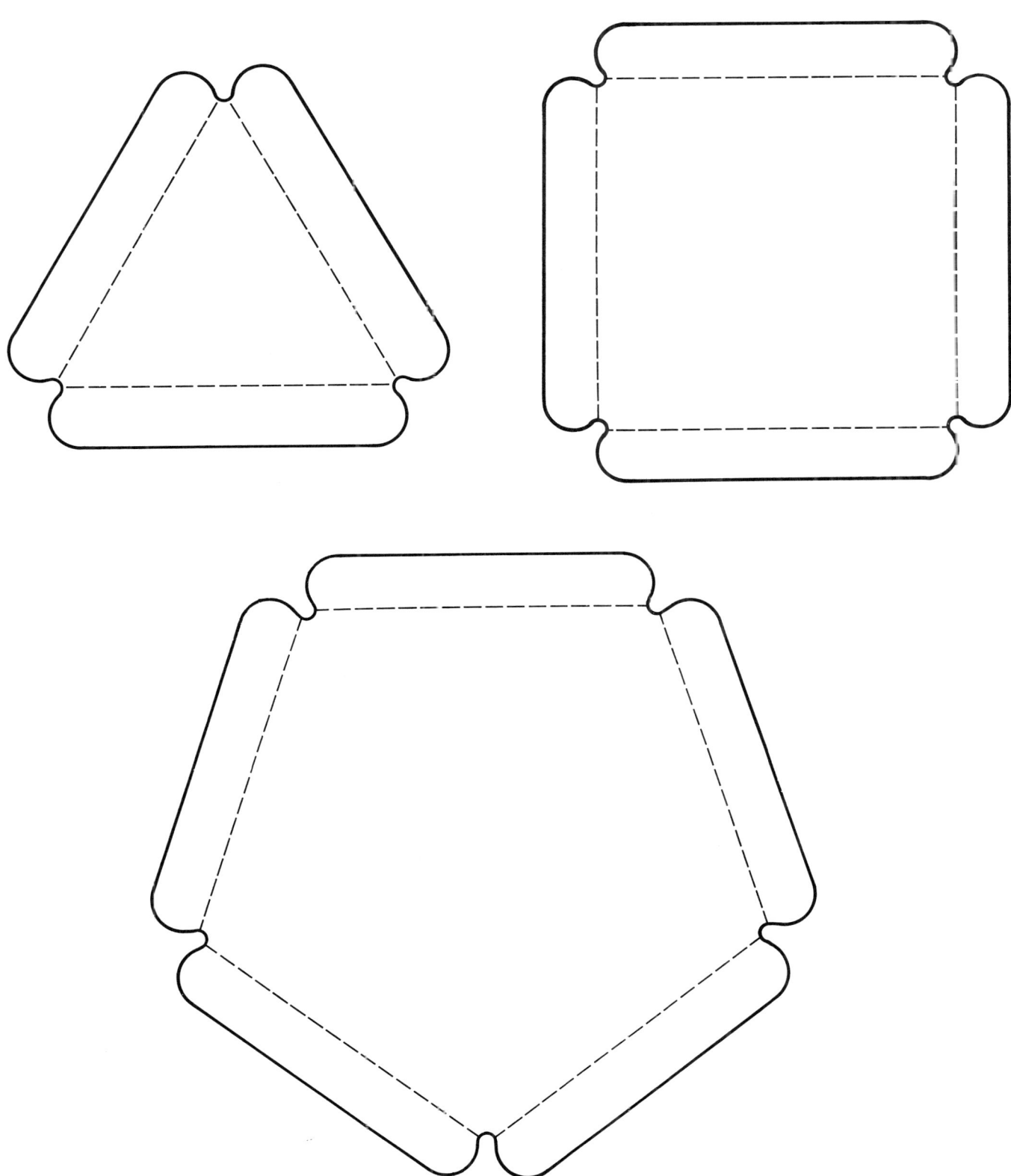

PROBLEM: The polyhedra that you have made have regular polygon faces of one type and all vertices are arranged alike. They are called *regular polyhedra*. There are only five convex regular polyhedra in all. Make an example of the remaining two. (Hint: They both have equilateral triangular faces.)

All rights reserved. Addison-Wesley Publishing Company

61 CONSTRUCTING SEMIREGULAR POLYHEDRA

A polyhedron with regular polygon faces of two or more types, with each vertex surrounded alike, is called a *semiregular polyhedron*.

Together with the square cutouts of the previous investigation, use the hexagon pattern below as a template for posterboard cutouts to make (by attaching cutouts with rubber bands) a semiregular polyhedron with six square faces and eight hexagon faces. This polyhedron is called a *truncated octahedron*.

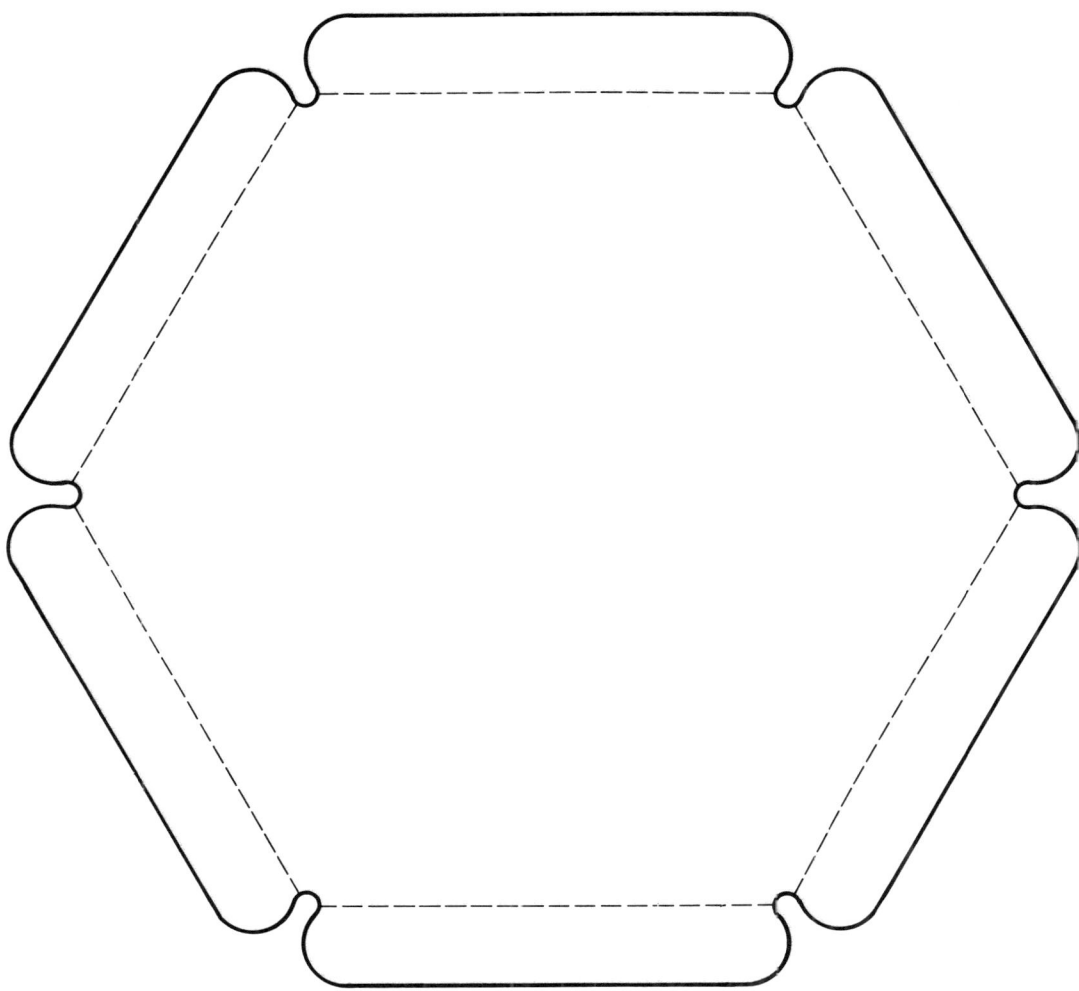

PROBLEM: There are 14 semiregular polyhedra in all. Experiment with the triangle, square, pentagon, and hexagon cutouts and make two more semiregular polyhedra. When you add the number of faces to the number of vertices for these polyhedra, do you get a number two less than the number of edges?

All rights reserved. Addison-Wesley Publishing Company

62 CONSTRUCTING DELTAHEDRA

A convex polyhedron with equilateral triangular faces only is called a *deltahedron*. There are only eight deltahedra and they contain 4, 6, 8, 10, 12, 14, 16, and 20 faces.

Use the pattern below as a template for posterboard cutouts and make an example of each of these polyhedra (attaching cutouts with rubber bands).

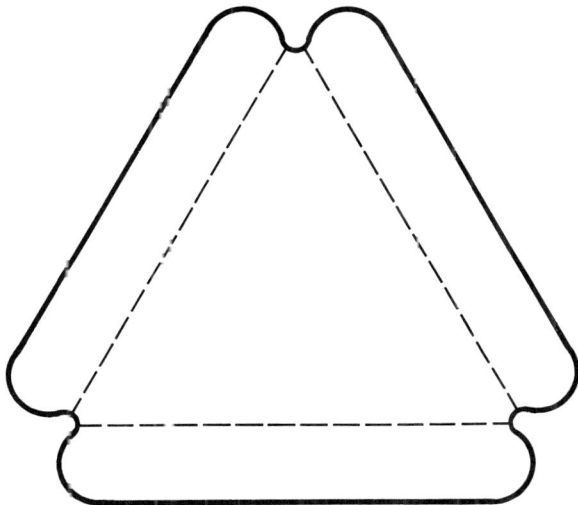

PROBLEM: Why do five of the eight deltahedra fail to be regular polyhedra?

63 POP-UP DODECAHEDRON

1. Use the net below as a template and cut from posterboard two copies of it. Crease along the edges of *ABCDE*.
2. Place the nets upon one another, one rotated 36° about the center point.
3. Weave an elastic band alternately above and below the corners as shown in the sketch below.
4. Raise your hand and watch the model pop up into a dodecahedron.

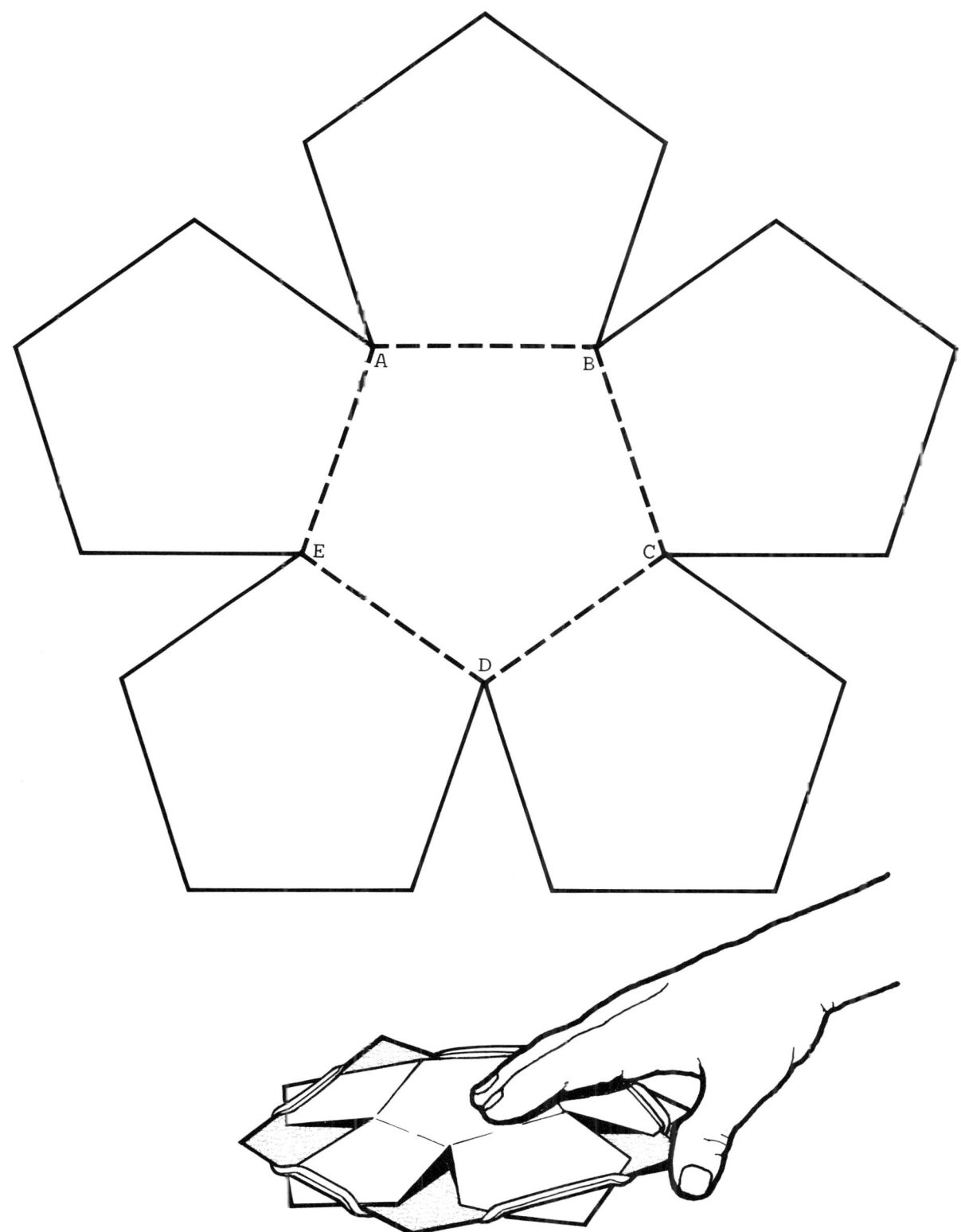

All rights reserved. Addison-Wesley Publishing Company

64 CONSTRUCTING A TETRAHEDRON

Construct a tetrahedron by following the instructions.

1. Cut out the rectangle below and fold along edge AD so that point C is facing you. Tape the edges AB together and edges BE together.
2. Fold along edges AC and BC back and forth in both directions.
3. Pinch the envelope so that points D and E are joined and C and C' are separated. Tape along edge CC' and the tetrahedron has been completed.

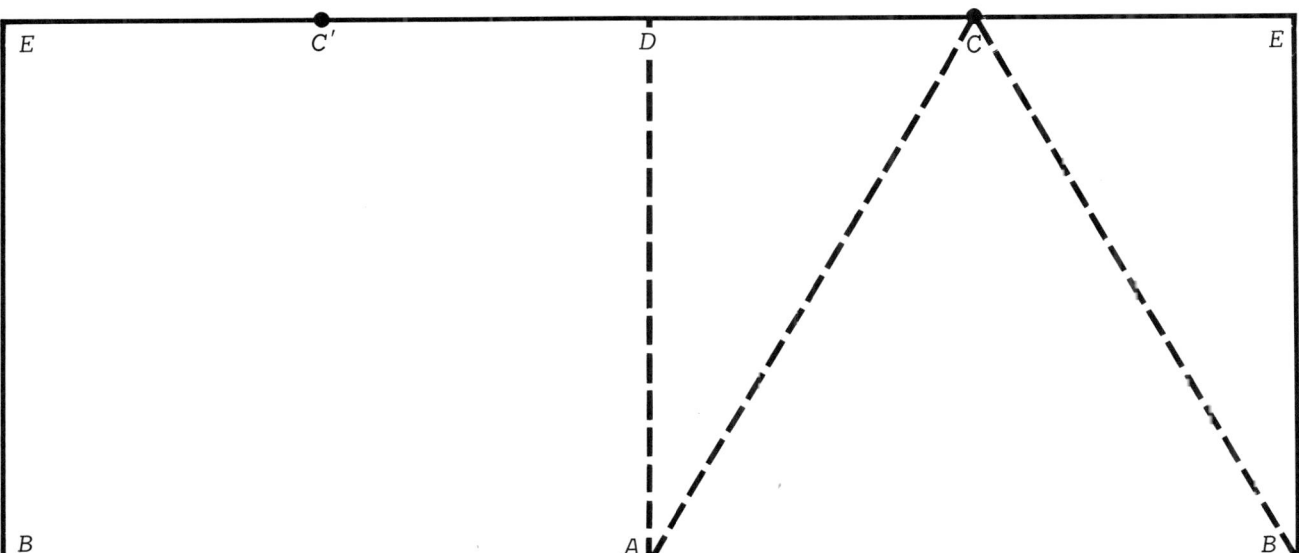

65 OPPOSITE VERTICES, EDGES, AND FACES FOR POLYHEDRA

For each of the regular convex polyhedra it is possible to identify examples of opposite vertices, opposite edges, and opposite faces. These concepts are illustrated here for a cube.

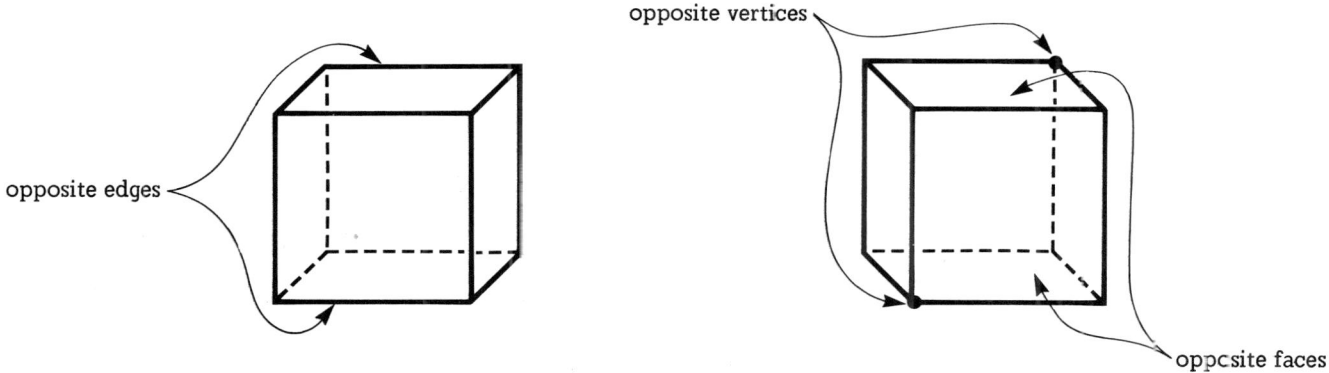

On pages 101-105 find nets for the five regular convex polyhedra. Construct each of these polyhedra and fill in the table below.

	How many pairs of opposite vertices?	edges?	faces?
tetrahedron			
cube			
octahedron			
dodecahedron			
icosahedron			

PROBLEM: If E represents the total number of edges of a polyhedron, F the total number of faces, and V the total number of vertices, what is the relationship between $F + V$ and E? (This relationship is known as Euler's formula.)

66 SYMMETRY OF THE CUBE

How many planes of symmetry does the cube possess? How many axes of rotational symmetry?

1. Draw one plane of symmetry on each cube until all the planes of symmetry are illustrated.
2. There are three types of rotational symmetry for the cube—180°, 120°, and 90°.
   Draw an axis of symmetry illustrating each of the three types.

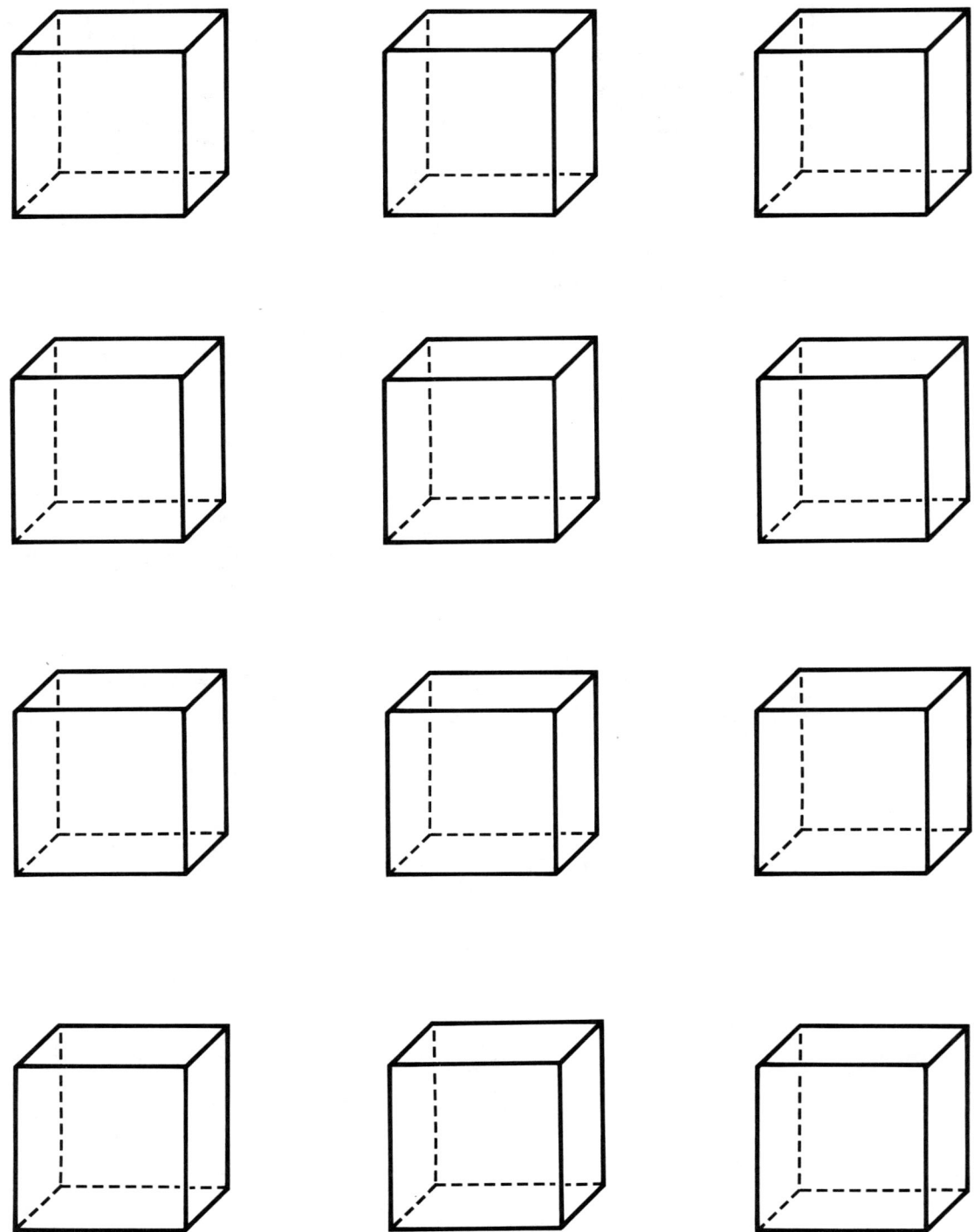

67 TETRAHEDRON, CUBE, OCTAHEDRON

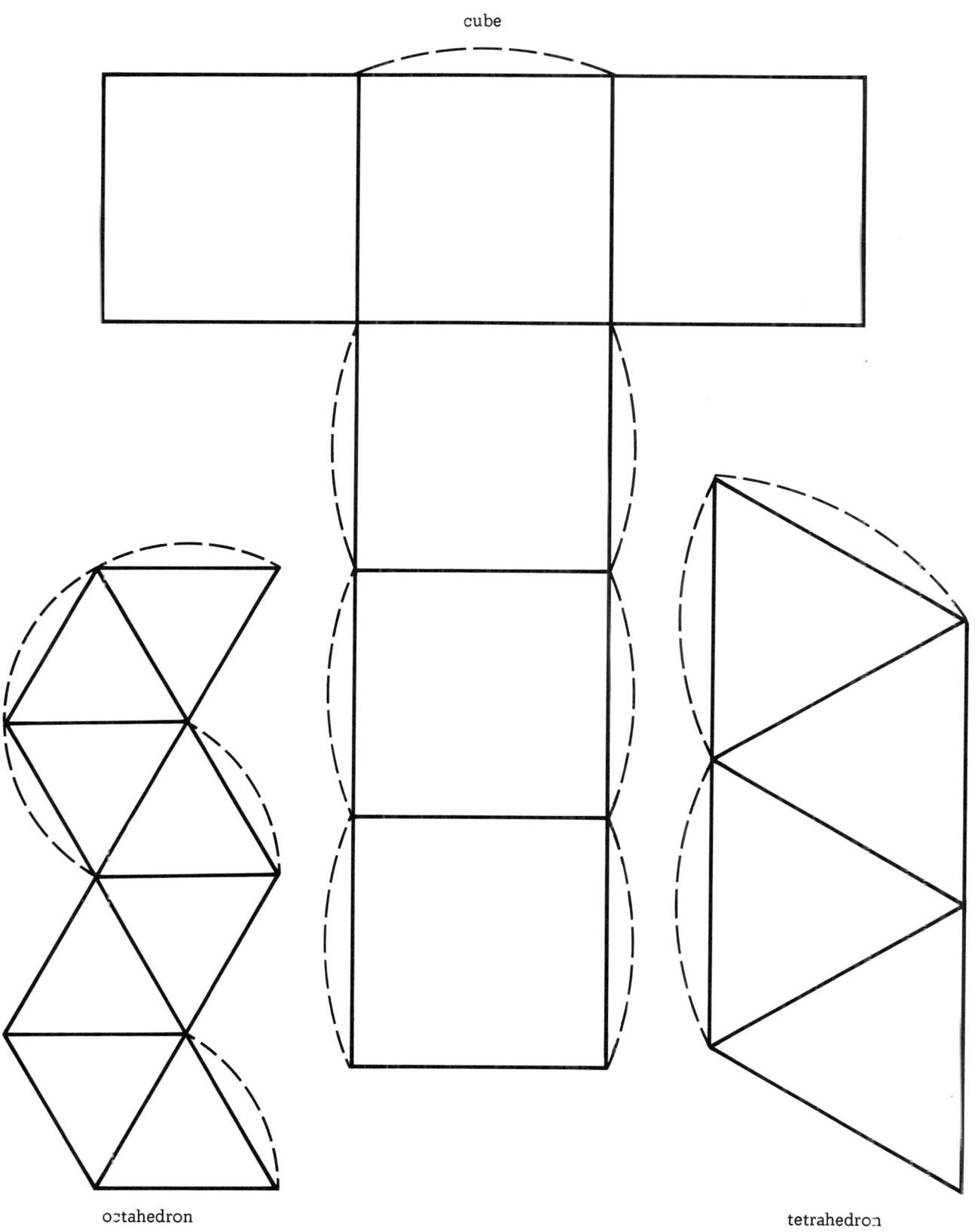

68   DODECAHEDRON

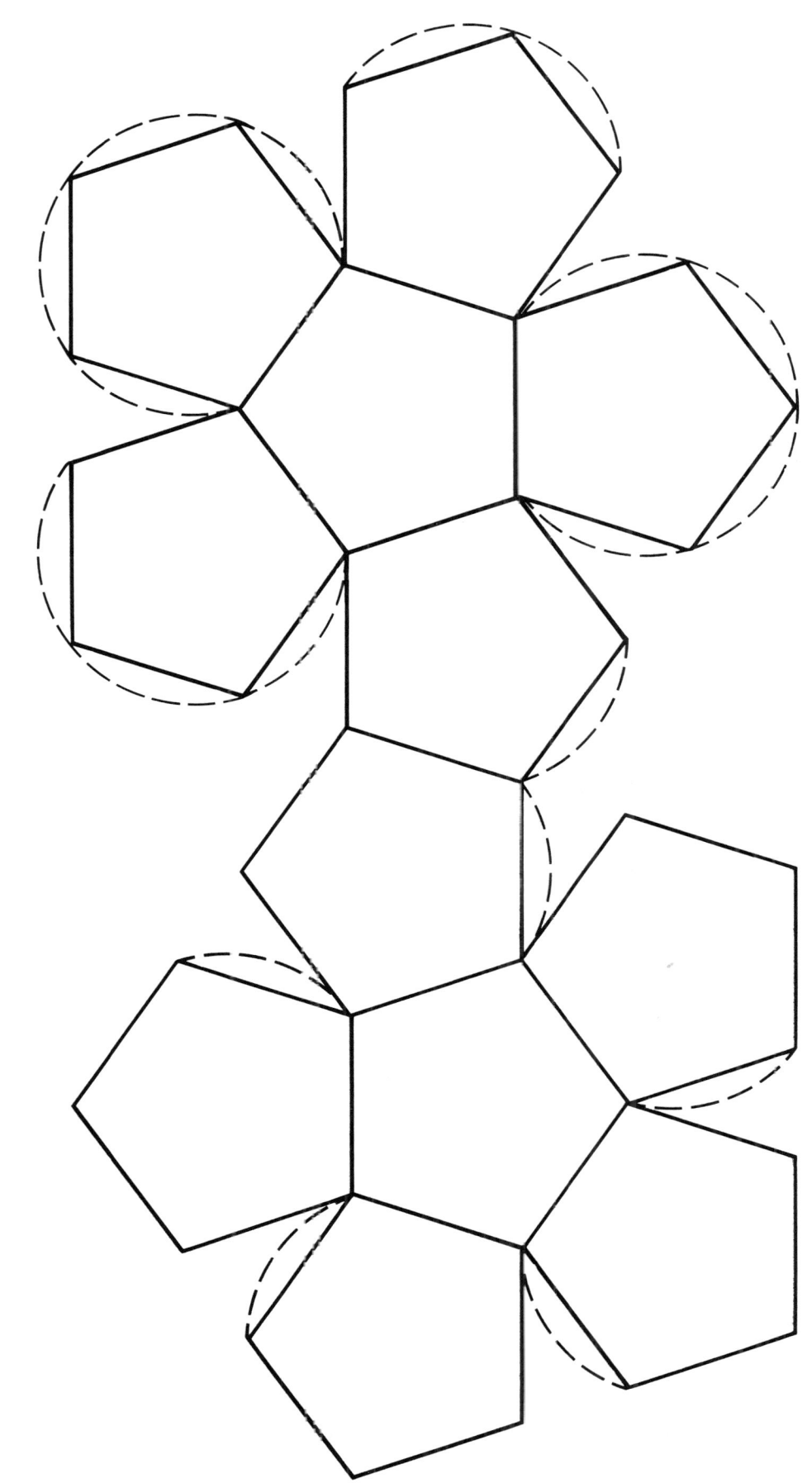

69 ICOSAHEDRON

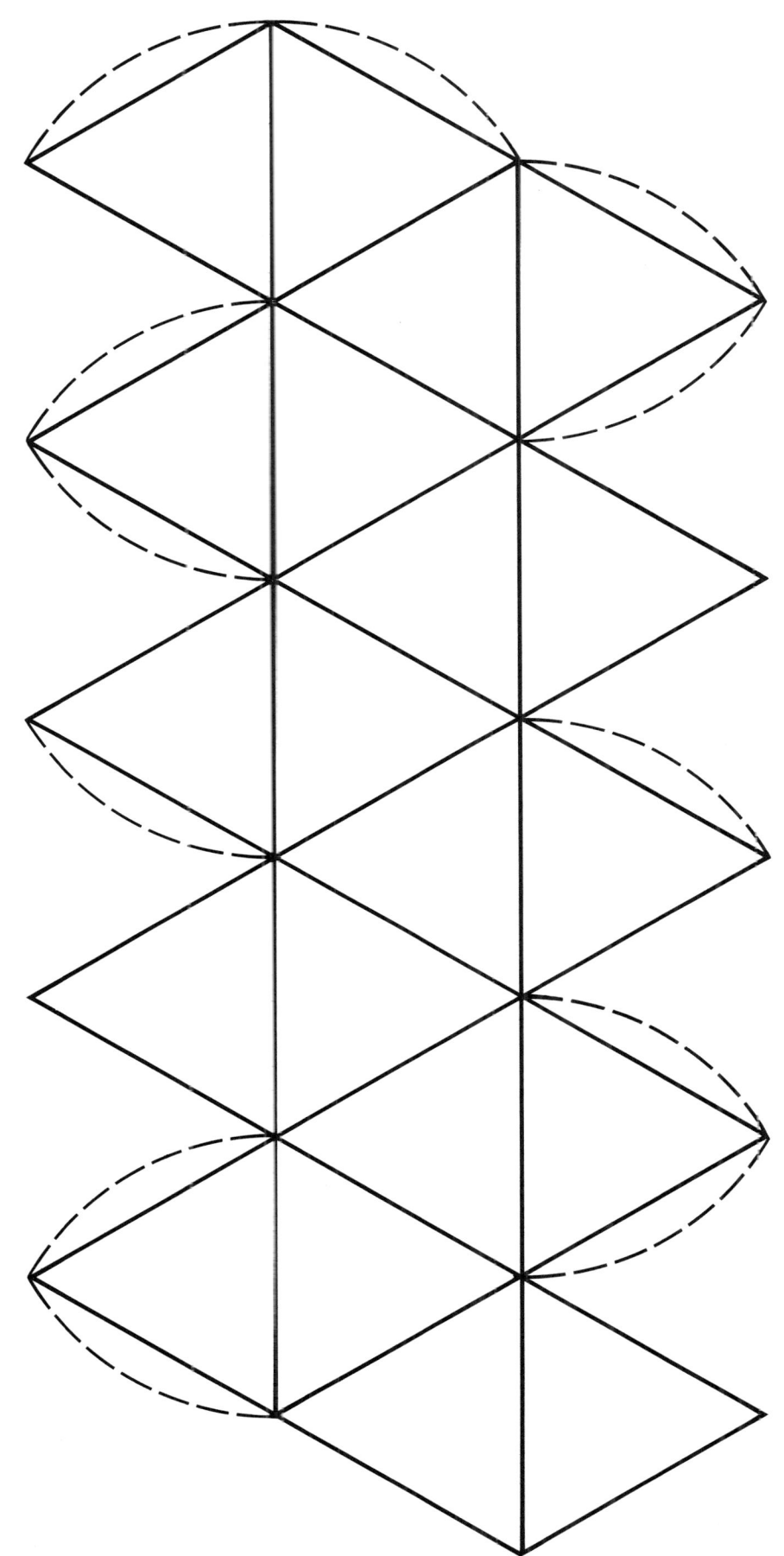

70 TETRAHEDRON PUZZLE

Make two copies of the nets below and construct the polyhedra from each of them. Can you place these two polyhedra together to form a tetrahedron?

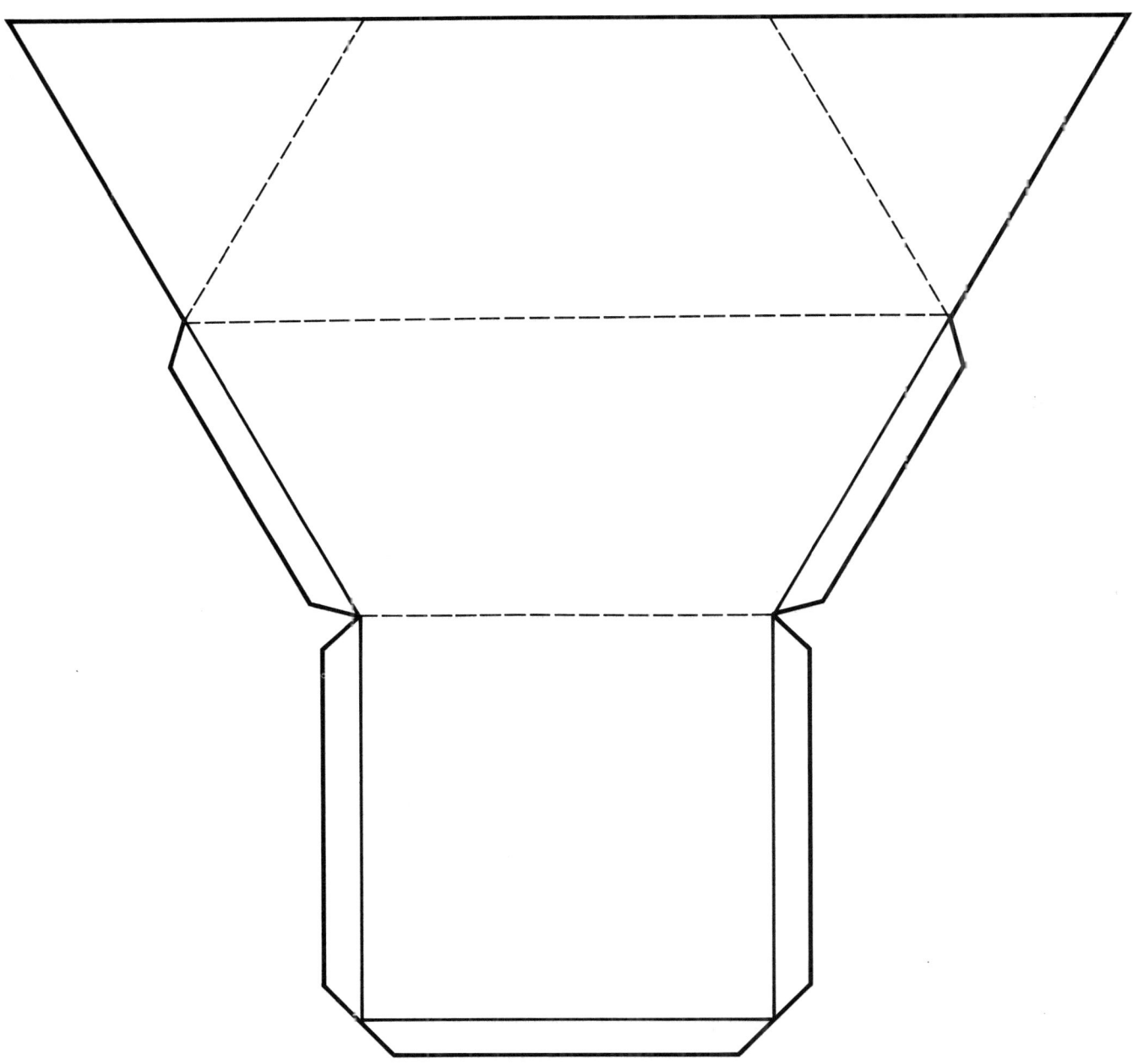

71 CUBE PUZZLE

Make two polyhedra with the net below. What polyhedra can be made by fitting two of these polyhedra together?

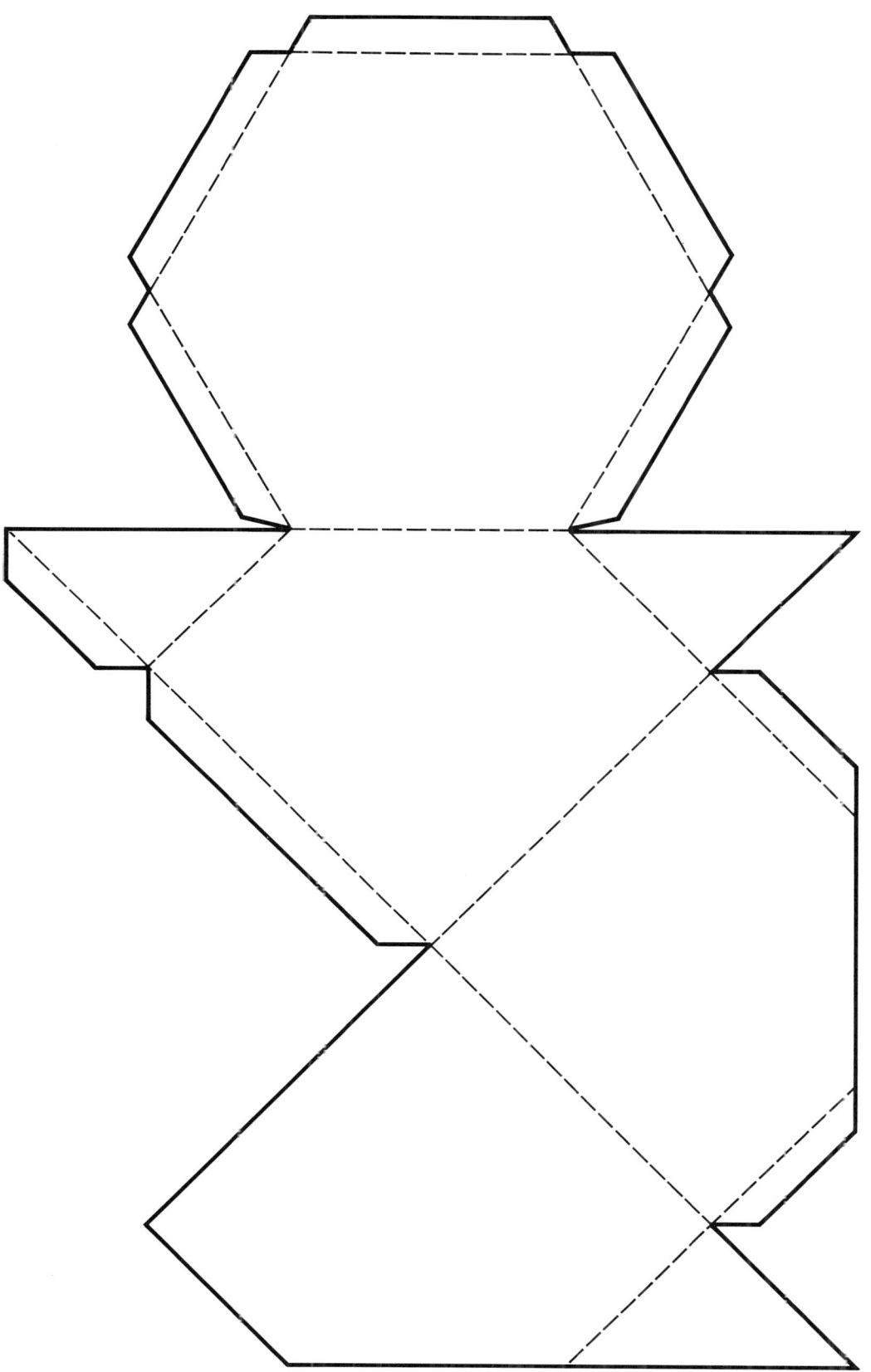

72   MIRA CONSTRUCTIONS

The top of the Mira is different from the bottom of the Mira since the bottom has an angled drawing edge. The angled side should always be toward you.

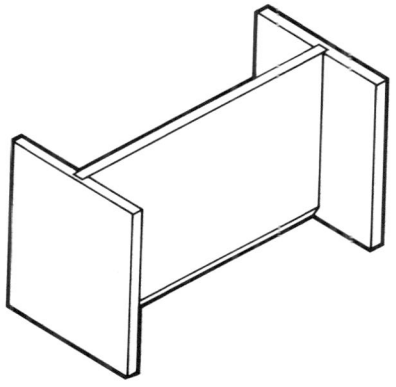

Draw the reflection image of the segment, angle, and triangles, reflected through the broken line.

(Place the Mira along the broken line, view the reflection in the Mira, and reach around the back of the Mira and trace the reflection images.)

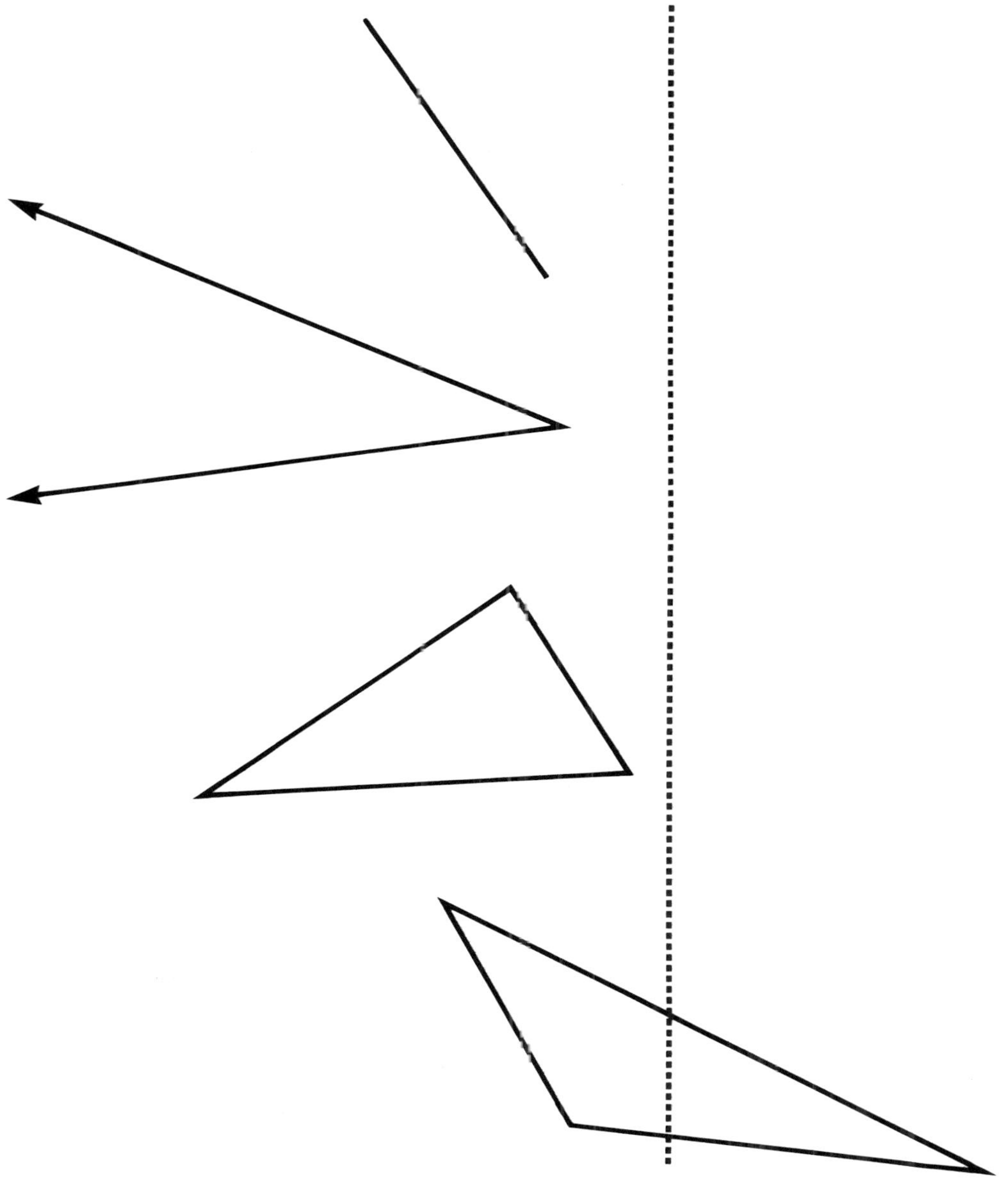

73 MIRA CONSTRUCTIONS

Use the Mira to construct each of the following.

A. Perpendicular bisector of segment AB

(Place the Mira on segment AB in such a way that the visual image of point A is on point B. Draw along the drawing edge of the Mira to produce the perpendicular bisector.)

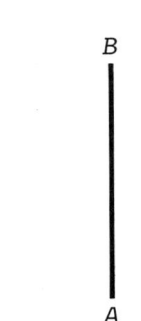

B. Bisector of angle ABC

(Place the Mira with point B on the drawing edge in such a way that the visual image of ray BC is on ray BA. Draw along the drawing edge of the Mira to produce the angle bisector.)

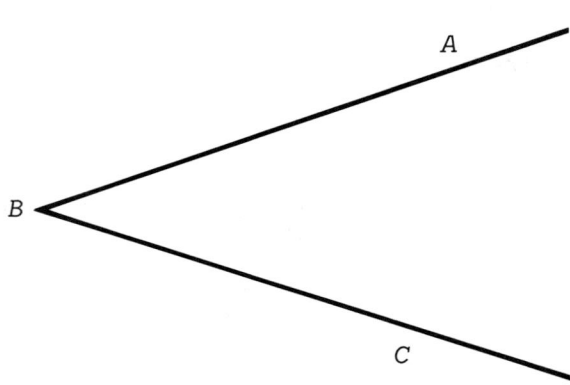

C. Perpendicular to a line through a point on the line

(Place the Mira with the drawing edge next to P in such a way that the visual image of half of the line is exactly on the other half of the line. Draw along the drawing edge to produce the perpendicular bisector of line 1.)

D. Perpendicular to a line through a point not on the line

(Place the Mira with the drawing edge next to P in such a way that the visual image of the half of line 1 in front of the Mira is exactly on the half of line 1 that is behind the Mira. Draw along the drawing edge to produce the perpendicular bisector of line 1.)

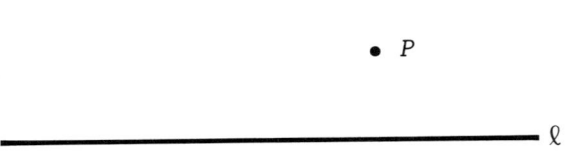

74 PRODUCTS OF REFLECTIONS (FLIPS)

For each case below use a Mira or compass and straight edge to draw the reflection image $P'Q'R'$ in line r of triangle PQR and then draw the reflection image $P''Q''R''$ in line s of triangle $P'Q'R'$.

In each case describe a single motion which is equivalent to the product of the two flips.

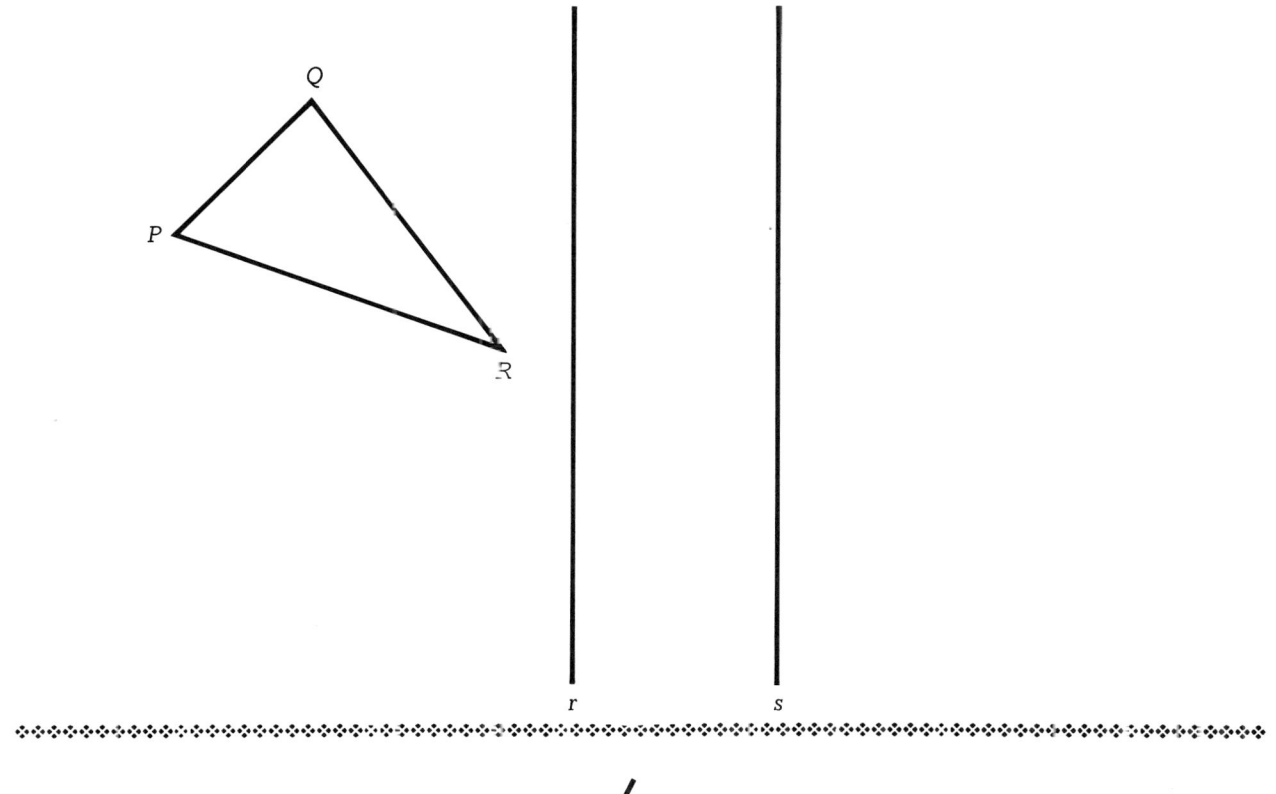

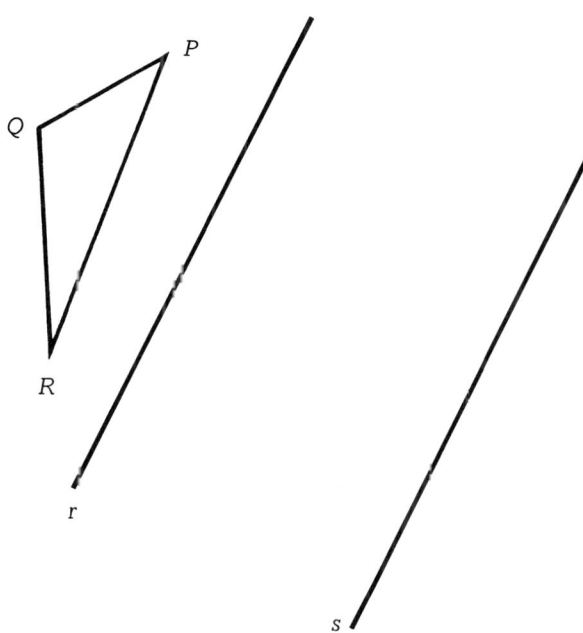

PROBLEM: What is the relationship between the distance between the two parallel lines and the resulting single motion?

All rights reserved. Addison-Wesley Publishing Company

75 PRODUCTS OF REFLECTIONS (FLIPS)

For each case below use a Mira or compass and straight edge to draw the reflection image $P'Q'R'$ in line r of triangle PQR and then draw the reflection image $P''Q''R''$ in line s of triangle $P'Q'R'$.

In each case describe a single motion which is equivalent to the product of the two flips.

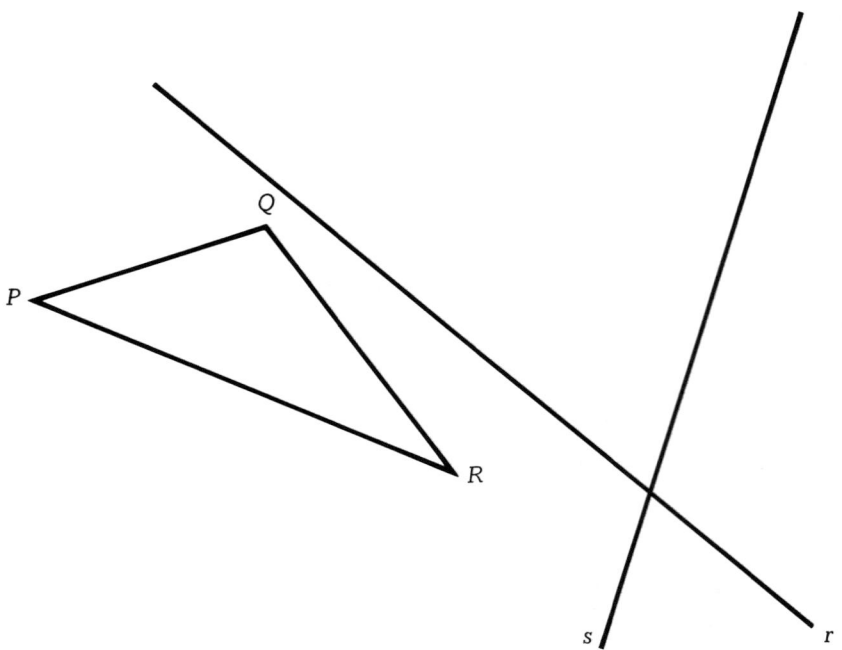

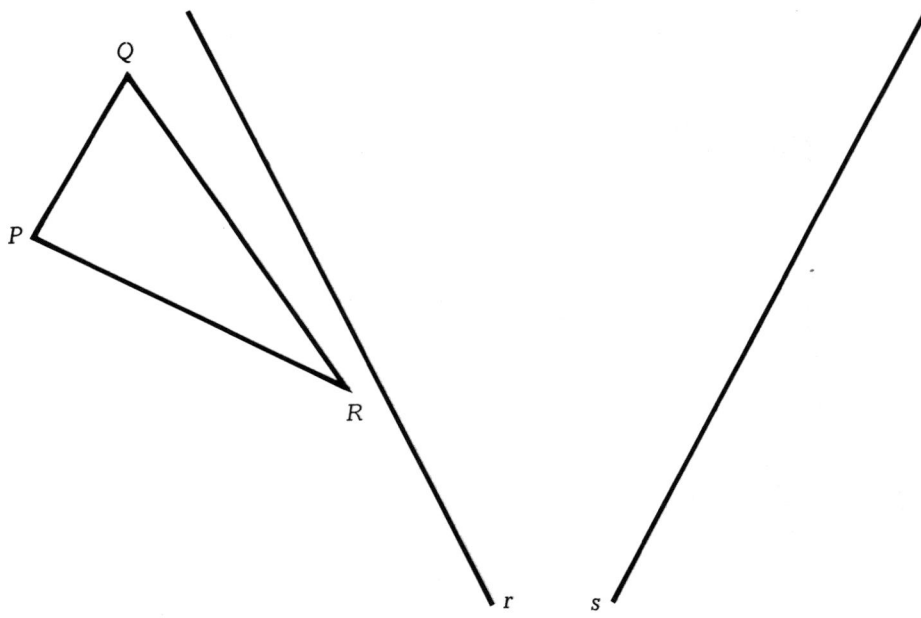

PROBLEM: What is the relationship between the angle measure of the acute angle between lines r and s and the resulting single motion?

76 PRODUCTS OF REFLECTIONS (FLIPS)

In each case below find a line *s* so that the reflection in line *r* followed by the reflection in line *s* maps one triangle onto the other.

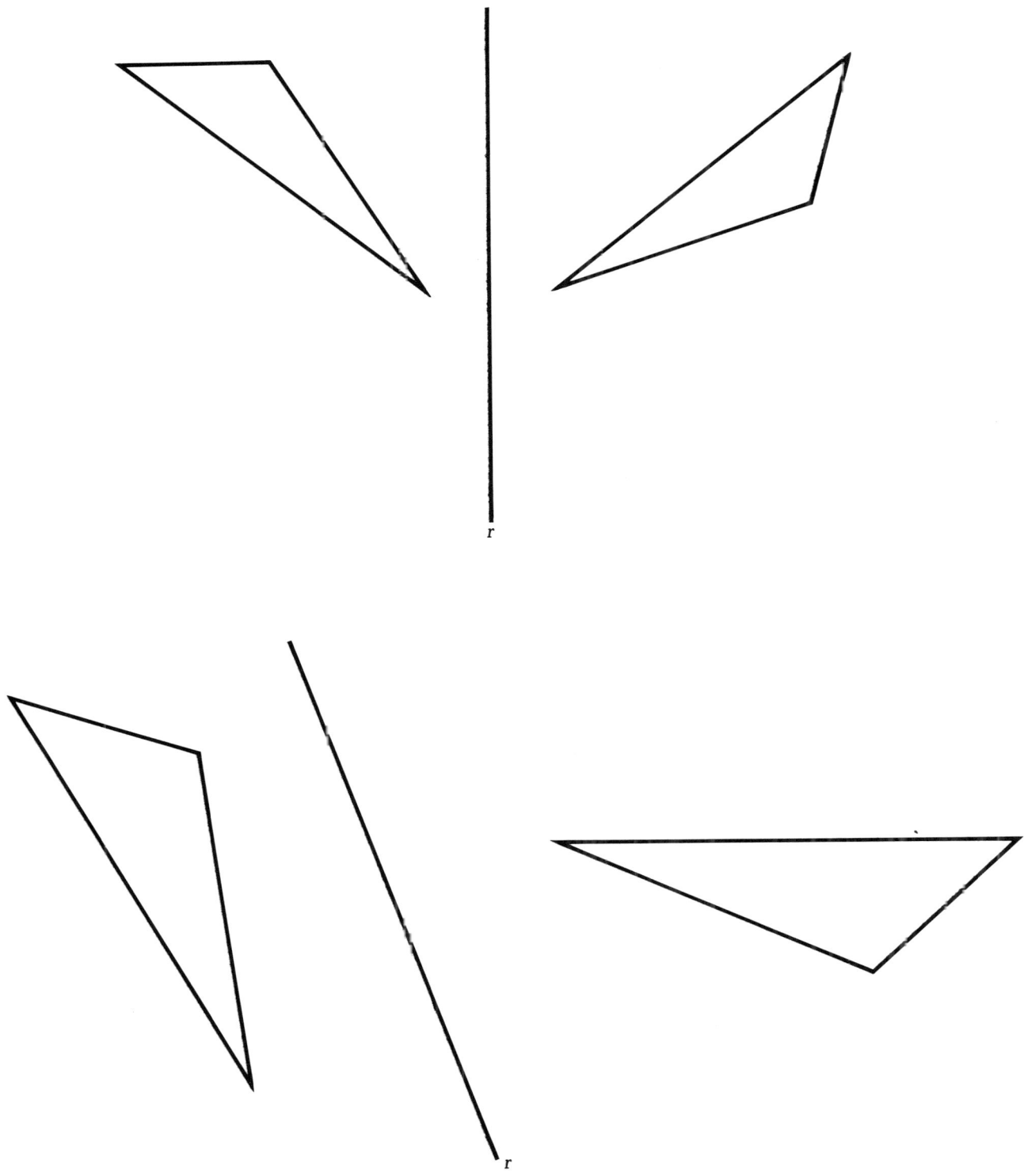

PROBLEM: In the above cases could the given line *r* have been selected differently? Experiment with the triangle pairs on the back of this page and see!

76 PRODUCTS OF REFLECTIONS (FLIPS) *(continued)*

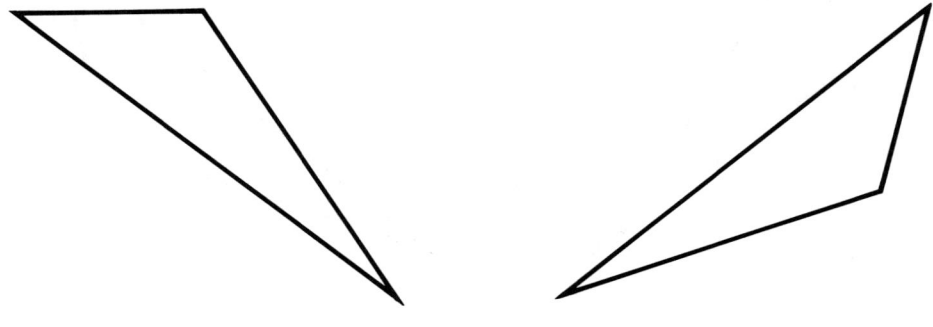

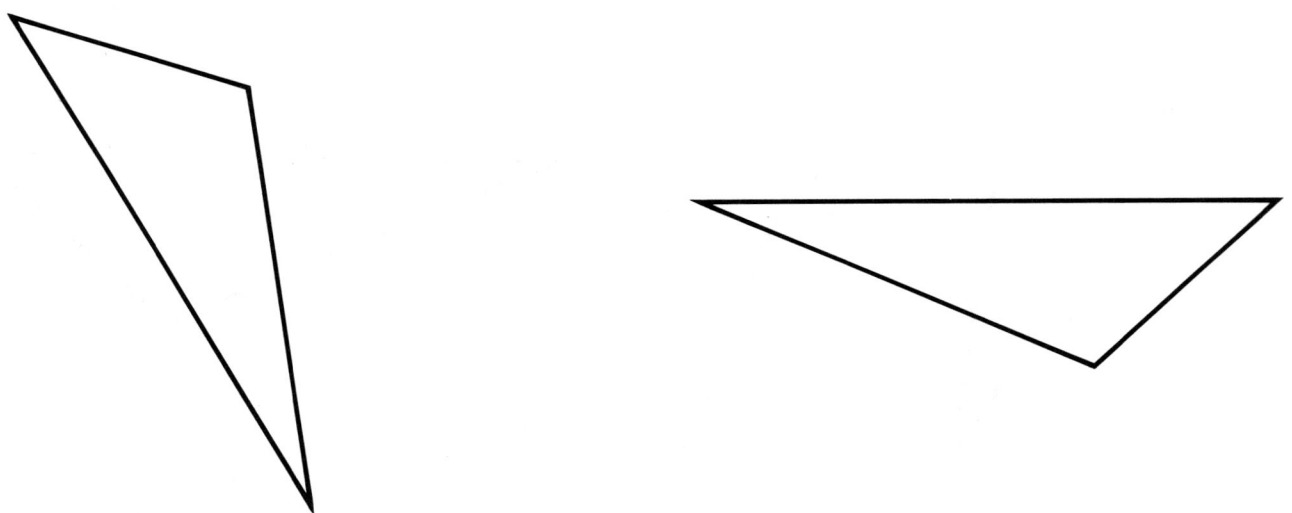

77 PRODUCTS OF REFLECTIONS (FLIPS)

In each case below find lines s and t so that the reflection in line r followed by the reflection in line s followed by the reflection in line t maps one triangle onto the other.

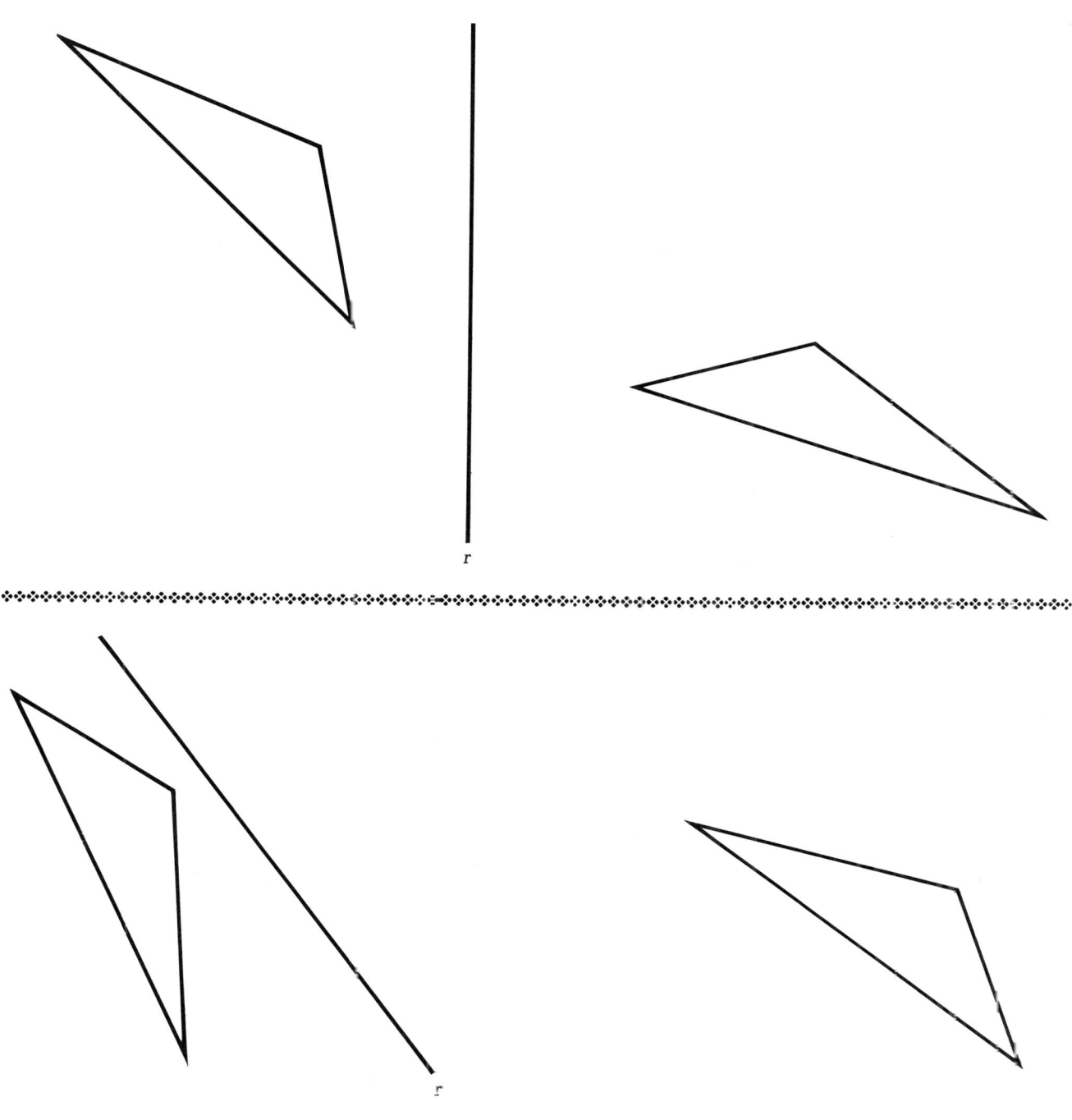

PROBLEM: In the above cases could the given line r have been selected differently? Experiment with the triangle pairs on the back of this page and see!

All rights reserved. Addison-Wesley Publishing Company

77 PRODUCTS OF REFLECTIONS (FLIPS) (continued)

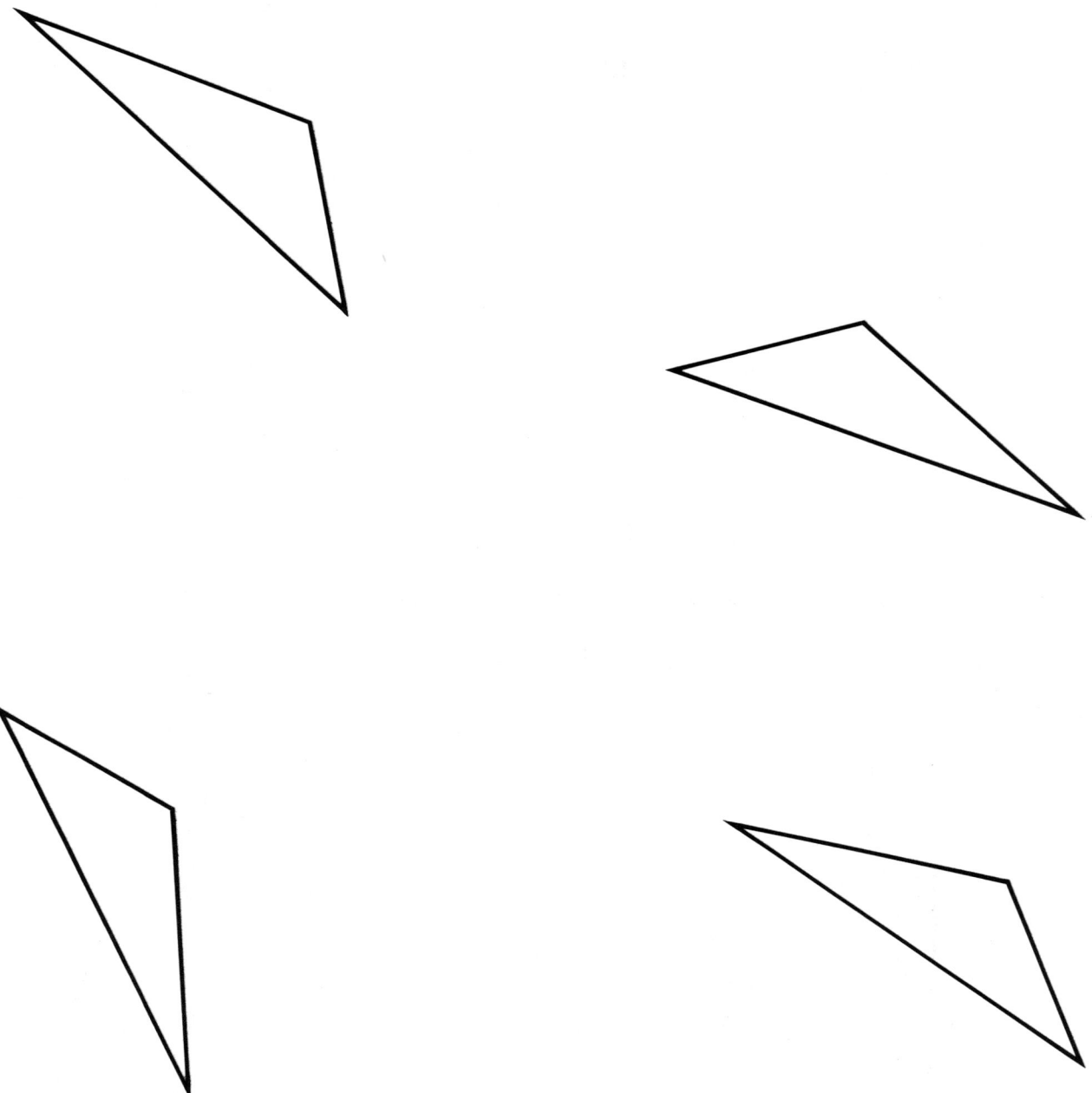

118

78 MOBIUS BAND

Cut out one of the strips, give one end a half twist, and join the ends together with tape. (Point A will match up with point D, and point B will match with C.)

You have just made a Mobius Band.

1. Color the edge of the Mobius Band until you return to the beginning point. What does this tell you about the number of edges on a Mobius Band?

2. Punch a hole in the surface of the band with a sharp object. Label the entrance of the point X and the exit of the point Y.

   Draw a continuous line (without crossing the edge) from X to Y. What does this tell you about the number of sides to the band?

3. In the middle of the band draw a line; cut the band in half by cutting along this line. Predict the outcome. Then cut.

4. Make a second Mobius Band. Cut along a line one third of the distance from the edge. Predict the outcome, then cut.

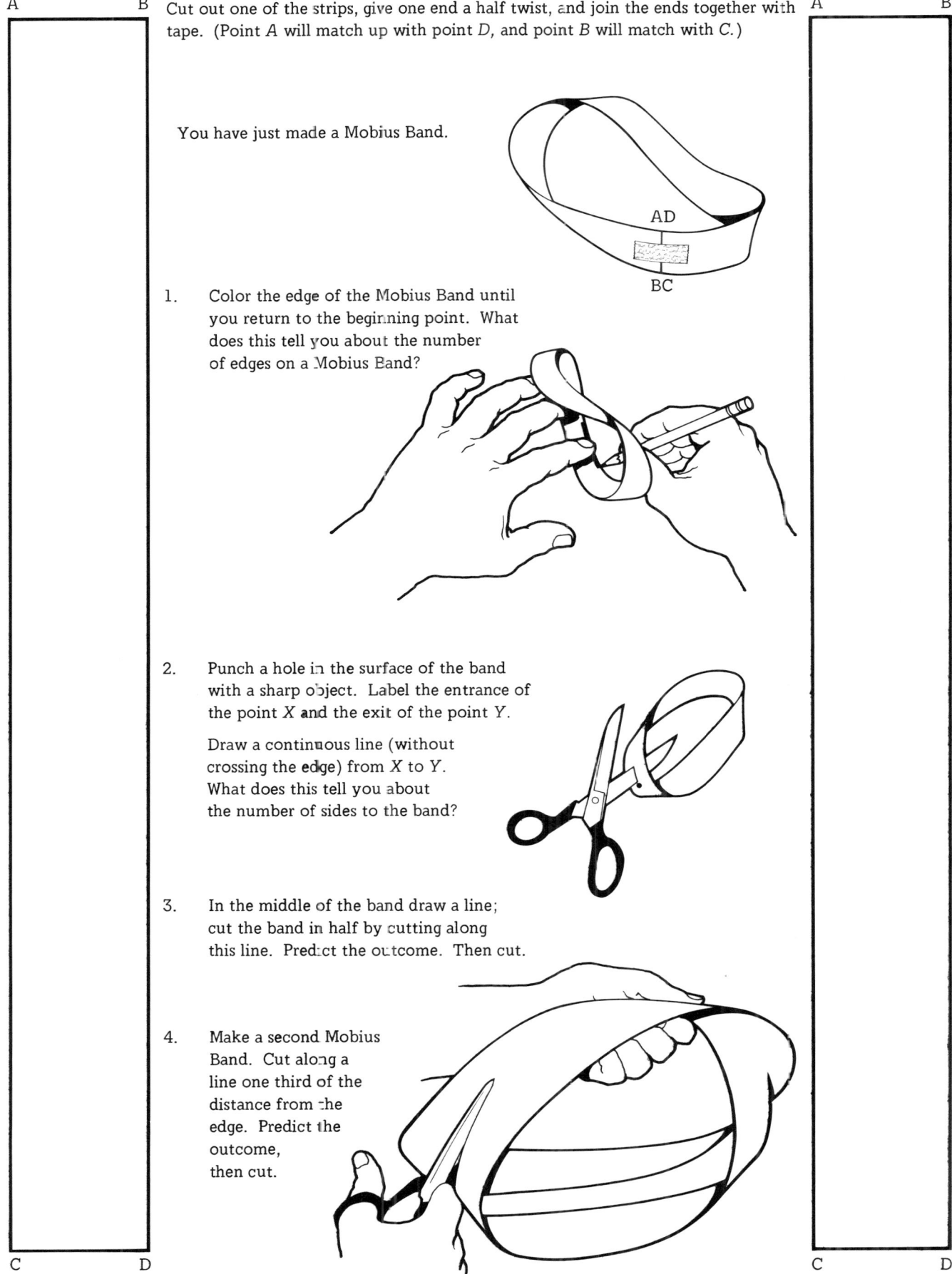

All rights reserved. Addison-Wesley Publishing Company

79   MISSING UNIT

The square below with area 8 x 8 = 64 square units has been dissected into a pair of congruent triangles and a pair of congruent quadrilaterals.

Cut out these four polygons and arrange them to cover the rectangle below.

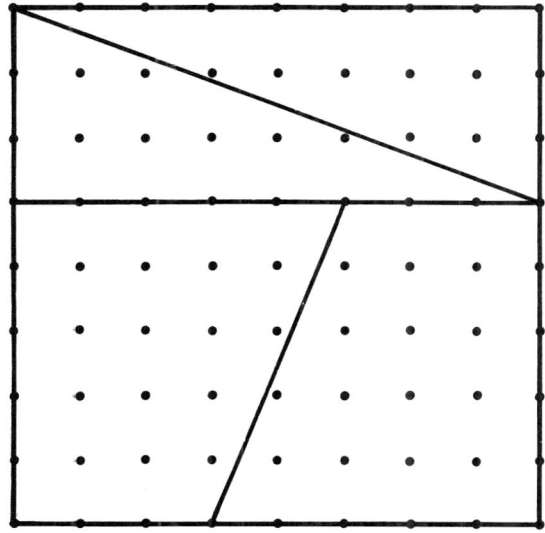

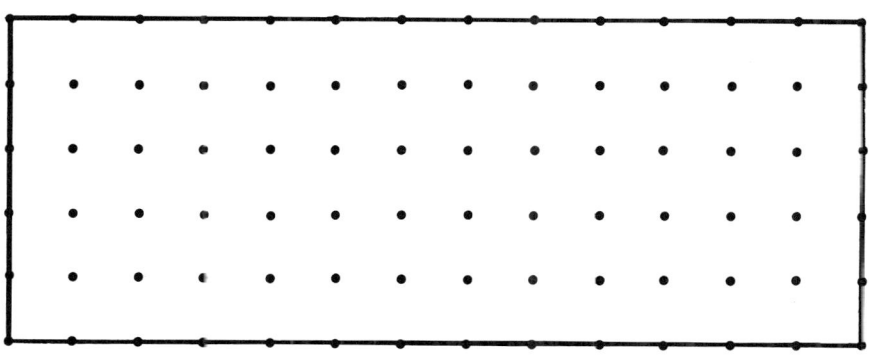

PROBLEM: Note that the area of the rectangle is 5 x 13 = 65. The area of the original square is 64. Where did the extra unit come from?

All rights reserved. Addison-Wesley Publishing Company